The Complete
Home Buyer's Bible

THE COMPLETE HOME BUYER'S BIBLE

William J. Molloy

John Wiley & Sons, Inc.
New York • Chichester • Brisbane • Toronto • Singapore

Copyright © 1996 by William J. Molloy

Published by John Wiley & Sons, Inc.

This publication is designed to provide accurate and authoritative information in regard to the subject matter covered. It is sold with the understanding that the publisher is not engaged in rendering legal, accounting, or other professional services. If legal advice or other expert assistance is required, the services of a competent professional person should be sought.

Library of Congress Cataloging-in-Publication Data:

Molloy, William J., 1947–
    The complete home buyer's bible. / William J. Molloy.
      p.   cm.
    Includes index.
    ISBN 0-471-13110-5 (cloth : alk. paper).—ISBN 0-471-13111-3
(pbk. : alk. paper)
    1. House buying—Handbooks, manuals, etc. 2. House construction—
Handbooks, manuals, etc. I. Title.
HD1379.M645 1996
643'.12—dc20   95-17416

Printed in the United States of America

10 9 8 7 6 5 4

CONTENTS

PREFACE

For more than 23 years, I have lived and worked in the real estate world. In 1971 my sister, a licensed real estate broker, insisted that I take the exam for my salesman's license, "just in case something comes along."

From that moment to the present, I have earned my personal Ph.D. (Paid His Dues) degree from the Street University, School of Hard Knocks, through on-the-job training. I became a dreamer and a builder of dreams.

Throughout the years, I've gained experience as a licensed real estate salesman, a licensed real estate broker, and a commercial mortgage broker. I went on to manage, buy, build, and sell multi-family projects of more than 200 homes and then began my career building single-family homes.

To date, I have negotiated, designed, developed, and sold several subdivisions; bought and sold more than 150 building lots; and helped to design, build, and sell more than 100 new homes.

In all of that time, every time, I've achieved a wonderful satisfaction in realizing my dreams, helping others to realize their dreams, and experiencing the excitement of actually owning a piece of the earth.

This book is the culmination of my experiences. I pass them on to you to help you fulfill your dreams.

I would like to thank the following people who have helped and encouraged me to write this book and offer my appreciation to them in this small way: Carolyn Molloy (my partner in life and also licensed in real estate for 17 years), for endlessly editing; Marc Molloy (my son), for always asking; Marilyn Molloy, for encouraging me to dream; Ron Reid, for editing; Paul Ornstein (my attorney and longtime friend), for his enthusiasm; Anne Julian (a longtime friend), for her invaluable advice; Jay Paggi (my engineer and longtime friend), for the technical help; Pat Koerber Bombardieri, for her honest opinions; Bob and Ann Mullen, for their expert research abilities, and especially Mike Hamilton, Senior Editor for John Wiley and Sons, for his enthusiasm and honesty.

INTRODUCTION

Buying real estate is an evolutionary process that begins with an idea and ends with ownership. This requires the buyer to take one step at a time.

The Complete Home Buyer's Bible is the most comprehensive, easy-to-read, plain language, step-by-step guide you can buy. Read this book and you will learn how to locate, qualify, and purchase a resale home, second home, condo, co-op, or townhouse. You will learn about mortgaging and how to prequalify yourself before you walk out the door. You will learn not only which decisions you need to make but how to make the right ones. You will learn how to inspect a resale home, wells and septic systems, water tables, surveys, and more.

The Complete Home Buyer's Bible takes the stress out of the decision-making process by giving the buyer the information needed and explains how to use that information to make the right choices—one step at a time.

Refer to the corresponding chapter before you begin each step of the process, and you will find the entire process educational, exciting, and most of all, rewarding.

Throughout this book, I offer descriptions of my personal experiences, of problems I encountered in actual situations and how they were resolved. I also offer explanations for avoiding any confusion by doing your homework in advance.

The Complete Home Buyer's Bible will guide you through the maze of the professional terminology and explains how to beat the "paper monster."

Whether you are a first-time buyer, a repeat buyer, or a licensed sales agent, you will find this book an invaluable tool for your success. When you finish reading this book, you will know as much or more about the "housing" end of the real estate business than many of those working in the industry.

1

SHOULD I OR SHOULDN'T I?

WHAT IS REAL ESTATE?

Real estate is a combination of two words, *real*, which is defined as "that which has existence—not artificial or imaginary"—and *estate*, which is defined as "the degree, nature, and amount of one's lawful interest in a property."

We are born within it, we live out our lives scurrying on it, and eventually we will all become a part of it; but owing to society's needs for regulation, the concept of real estate can be difficult to understand.

When you own a patch of land with or without your home (or condo or co-op) sitting on it, you own a piece of the planet. Your ownership will include everything from the depths of the earth to the highest point in the sky. This is the most fascinating aspect of owning real estate; it is a mystery and an adventure. But to join this exclusive club of real estate owners, you must first become initiated by surviving the complicated maze of terminology and documentation.

Those of you who have been out of the buyers' market for a while and are considering reentering it will discover that the purchase process has changed considerably since the early 1980s—financing has changed as well as the laws governing property transfers. Building codes have changed; brokerage laws, zoning laws, environmental laws, banking credit applications, closing documents, and contract forms have also all changed.

There is a certain internal language related to any industry, but to understand the purchase process is to understand not only how this language is interpreted by the professionals but also how it applies to you. In this book you will gain an understanding of both of these important points.

You will earn many titles as you follow this maze, and you will be treated differently with each title change. You began your adventure as a dreamer, and because you have decided to act upon that dream, your new title is **prospective purchaser**.

A prospective purchaser, or prospect, is someone who has decided to buy. This decision is a powerful one and will affect many lives. When there is a sale, many people and institutions make money, such as the broker, sales agent, attorneys, bank, and title company, not to mention the state and the seller. When you enter a sales office, it is not the same as shopping in a department store; you are the catalyst to a process in which a lot of money will change hands.

Now that you are a prospective purchaser, it is time to join one of the two basic buyer groups and earn a new title. You will be considered either a **move-up (repeat) buyer** or a **first-time buyer**. Move-up buyers have already been through the maze at least once and thus have experience. They also know more about what they need and want in their next home and what to watch out for. First-time buyers do not have the same advantages and are actually at the mercy of their advisors.

RELOCATION

Corporate America is on the move because of downsizing and plant closings. Many companies are changing locations, and employees are either moving with their current employer or searching for new employment in other areas. Gone are the days when children grew up in the same neighborhood as had their parents, raised their own children, and then settled into the community. It used to be that people simply wished to relocate; now they often have to.

If you are being relocated by your employer, you now have another title, **relocation purchaser**. When relocation purchasers walk into a real estate office, they inform the sales professionals that they have a job, they can afford the financing, and they not only want to but *have* to buy. Relocated buyers' time is limited owing to job requirements, and the sales professionals know that they have a limited time to locate and complete the sale. Just as in any other business, a buyer gets preferential treatment over someone who is just looking. A prospective purchaser is *interested* in buying; the relocation purchaser *has* to buy and will receive preferential treatment.

WHAT ARE THE FINANCIAL BENEFITS OF OWNING REAL ESTATE?

Whatever your reasons for moving may be, if you are a first-time buyer, buying a home requires a substantial financial commitment. It is an investment as well as a change of lifestyle.

If you are presently renting, your monthly payment covers the cost of your living space and occasionally includes certain utilities such as heat and hot water. The landlord takes care of maintaining the property, and you are able to quietly enjoy your space. You receive no tax benefits, and neither do you build equity or have total control over your living environment. For my money, the benefits of owning far outweigh the benefits of renting.

Equity

There are millions of apartments out there occupied by millions of people who rent as a matter of preference or affordability. However, when you rent, you are simply helping to pay off someone else's mortgage. If your preference is apartment-style living, at least consider buying a condominium or co-op. The monthly payments will reduce *your* mortgage; you will build equity and receive certain tax benefits as well.

Equity is the money value of a property in excess of any debts that can be held against it. Like any other industry, real estate is dominated by the laws of supply and demand. If the supply is great and the demand is low, prices and terms should be easier to obtain, and the reverse should apply if demand is high and the supply is low. Keep the laws of supply and demand in mind. Depending on the area of your search, understanding the local market can save you thousands of dollars in purchasing and financing your home.

Your rent payment is an investment in your lifestyle, not in the property. When you become a property owner, you are entitled to deduct certain property costs from your income taxes. Thus far, all interest charges and property taxes pertaining to your mortgage payment are fully tax deductible (see chapter 3). Because most of your mortgage payment will be interest in the early years of the loan, this deduction is substantial.

Appreciation

In New York State during the hectic mid-1980s, properties were appreciating annually at more than 20 percent of their original value. Those values are adjusting downward now owing to the area's economy. However, homes that were constructed in late 1977 that sold for $69,000 and appreciated to sell in the mid-1980s for $269,000 are still reselling today for $195,000—more than 2½ times their original value despite the economy. Buying a home is an investment that will give you tax benefits—as well as appreciation of your investment over time.

Tax Benefits

Let's see just how much you can save by owning as opposed to renting. The following example shows projected monthly and annual numbers for the mortgage's principal, interest, taxes, and insurance. First, however, we need to review some terms you'll need to understand: **adjusted gross income** and **tax bracket**. Your adjusted gross income is the amount of income you claim after all of your deductions have been taken out, and your tax bracket is the percentage of your adjusted gross income that you pay in income taxes annually.

Review last year's tax returns and locate your adjusted gross income. Then check to see how much you paid in *total* (federal, state, and local) income taxes. Divide the amount you paid in taxes by the adjusted gross income to arrive at your tax bracket. If your gross income was $45,000 and you had deductions totaling $2,000, your adjusted gross income would then be $43,000. If your total income taxes amounted to $16,340, then your tax bracket would be 38 percent, because $16,340 divided by $43,000 equals 0.38. (Because tax preparation is such an exact science, you should ask your accountant to calculate your tax bracket for you.)

The Big Picture

Inflation hurts us in many ways by eroding our buying power—and helps those of us who own real estate by making everything more expensive and thus more valuable. As we all know, inflation rates change over the years.

If you were thinking of buying a home in a specific area, you would contact the local tax assessor and ask about the various prices and taxes of sold homes in your target price range. Review Table 1.1 to see how you could break down the expenses by month and year. The property taxes and your tax bracket would probably be different, but the formula is the same. Then review Table 1.2 to see how those numbers could add up to sizable financial benefits for you each year.

If you consider all the tax benefits and add the appreciation in value, you can see that your actual housing costs would be very little, even with the current appreciation rate of 3 percent per year.

Table 1.1. Homeowner Expenses

Projected mortgage amount	$107,600.00
Estimated annual property taxes	$2,700.00
Life of mortgage loan	30 years
Projected interest rate	8%
Projected monthly insurance	$35.00
Estimated monthly property taxes	$225.00
Monthly principal and interest	$790.00
Principal, interest, taxes, and insurance (PITI)	1,050.00
Estimated purchaser tax bracket	38%
Estimated annual appreciation of property	+3%

Table 1.2. Homeowner Savings

Deductible interest the first year	$ 8,608.00
Deductible property taxes	2,700.00
Total interest and tax deductions	11,308.00
Deductible tax and interest reduces income tax by	4,297.04
Property value increase	3,228.00
First-year principal mortgage reduction	1,292.00
Total first-year financial benefits	8,817.04
Monthly financial benefits	734.75
Actual monthly house cost	315.25

By deducting the interest and taxes, you would create a saving in income taxes of $4,297. Your property would increase in value by $3,228, and you would reduce the mortgage debt by $1,292, thus increasing your equity in the property. Now add $8,817.04 to your current total annual rent and ask yourself how much it is really costing you to continue renting instead of owning. Not only do you receive these benefits, but you also own the home, and you are building equity in the property every month. You will receive that equity upon the sale of the home. When you think about it, unless you rent for the lifestyle, you cannot afford *not* to own a home.

THE SINGLE-FAMILY DETACHED HOME

Most home buyers prefer single-family detached homes. A detached home sits on its own private lot unattached to any other structure except possibly a garage or other building that services only that home.

The lot size will vary according to zoning requirements (see chapter 11), and the other lots in the surrounding area will usually be much the same size. When you buy a single-family detached home, you own the house as well as the lot the house sits on, and you are solely responsible for the upkeep of the entire property. You can change the house and grounds to suit your needs as long as you comply with local zoning, building codes, and deed restrictions if any (see chapter 11).

AMERICA ON THE MOVE

The problem with today's rapid movement of corporations and employees is that many of those moving will not stay put for the long haul. In previous years a home buyer could expect to work and live in the same area until retirement. In the 1990s, home buyers are no longer planning to own the same house for the long term.

Add to this corporate movement the desire of the repeat buyer to move up to a different or larger home, and you have a situation where the average buyer in the 1990s will only remain in his or her home for an average of five to seven years before again relocating.

Real estate markets change constantly in response to fluctuations in the national and local economy, even in areas that are presently depressed owing to plant closings or layoffs. Once the initial shock of the bad news settles down, a large number of homes appear on the market. Prices fall because the supply outweighs the demand. The best bargains are snatched up by local first-time home buyers who previously could not afford to do so, and soon buyers come in from other areas to take advantage of the remaining good deals. In a short time, only the less-desirable homes are still on the market. Buyers start looking into new construction, prices start to stabilize because of the increase in demand and diminishing supply, property begins to appreciate once again, and the recovery ball is rolling.

The best time to buy is when the market is depressed and prices are down; the worst time to buy is when the market is strong and prices are high.

2

WHAT DO I NEED?

Although there are many styles and floor plans for the construction of homes, there are but two basic forms of housing: detached and attached. The benefits—and resultant popularity—of detached homes were discussed in the previous chapter. **Attached homes** are exactly that, attached to another home or unit by shared common walls, ceilings, or floors. They are less expensive than detached homes and may be a good starting point for young people just getting into the housing game.

When a developer builds attached housing, the costs for the roads, water, sewer, drainage, and recreational and common areas are less than if the project was designed as a detached project, because the homes are clustered together. It is less expensive to build common walls and apply siding to each end of one building than it is to apply siding to each side of many buildings. By buying windows, doors, appliances, heating systems, and other items needed for construction in large bulk orders, the developer saves money. The savings are passed on to the individual buyer through lower prices.

There are several styles of attached homes, such as condominiums (condos), cooperatives (co-ops), and town houses. The previous descriptions do not describe the style of home as much as they describe the form of ownership.

CONDOMINIUMS

Condominium ownership offers you title to the interior of your living space, which is attached to your neighbors' by common walls, floors, or ceilings. You receive a deed to your unit, and you finance your purchase with an independent mortgage. You share the costs of maintaining common areas with the other owners. The common areas consist of hallways, parking lots, sidewalks, recreational areas, and all exterior areas including the walls and roofs of the project.

Condominiums can take the form of garden apartment–style buildings of two to three stories or of high-rise buildings. However, the term *condominium* refers to the **form of ownership** rather than the **style of construction**, so almost any type of project can be organized as a condominium.

The common areas are owned and maintained by a **homeowners association** (HOA) that is organized and filed with the state as a corporation. The HOA has a **charter** that states what it as a corporation will do and must establish **bylaws**, which are regulations concerning the operation of the property. The homeowners association has an elected board of directors that oversees the running of the project, authorizes repairs, and collects the dues or maintenance fees from each owner. In many projects, the managing of the project is contracted to a professional management company, with the homeowners association's board of directors remaining as the final decision makers.

The advantage of sharing maintenance costs with other condo owners is that someone else will take care of the cleaning, grass cutting, and snow shoveling. The disadvantage is that you will be subject to the restrictions adopted by the homeowners association, which may apply to such things as style of windows, paint colors of hallway doors, and pets. You must decide if this form of ownership is right for you. Will you mind living close to your neighbors, or do you like to play your stereo at high volume? Although you will have voting rights as a member of the HOA, your voice is only one of many.

When considering buying a condo, obtain a copy of the **articles of incorporation**, **bylaws**, **declaration of covenants, conditions and restrictions**, and **house regulations**. This information will answer questions about pets, rental of the unit, and changes in exterior decor and will tell you how the entire project operates.

COOPERATIVES (CO-OPS)

Cooperative ownership, like condominium ownership, involves sharing financial responsibility for the operating expenses of the entire property with one major difference. Instead of buying the actual title to your living space, **you buy shares in the corporation that owns the property**. You are also provided with a property lease indicating your right of possession of your unit. Thus, your actual ownership is not considered ownership of the real estate.

The disadvantages of cooperative ownership are the same as those of condo ownership except that in a cooperative, a single mortgage loan is taken out by the corporation. If any shareholder fails to pay his or her share of the financing, the other shareholders must make up the difference. Also, the purchase of shares in a cooperative must be approved by a majority of the shareholders.

If you're considering moving into a co-op, talk with several of the current owners to get a feel for how well the project is managed. Ask about the response time for repairs and how often the project is cleaned. Check the exterior grounds to get an idea of how well the exterior of the project is maintained (see chapter 6). Verify that the maintenance fees are stable and not increasing every year to pay for improvements.

TOWN HOUSES

The most popular form of attached housing, a town house is as close as you can get to a detached single-family home and still be attached to another home by a common wall. Ownership of a town house, also known as **deed-out** or **fee-simple** ownership, gives you a deed not only to your section of the building but also to the property in front and in back of the building. If your unit is on the end of the building, you will also own the side yard, just as you would if you owned a detached home. Fee-simple ownership offers several advantages. You have the **exclusive right of possession**, in other words, complete control of the property.

You have the **right of quiet enjoyment**, which means you can use the property in any manner you choose consistent with local laws. You also have the **right of disposition**, which allows you to use the property throughout your lifetime or to sell or will it to others as you see fit.

The town house is similar to the other forms of attached housing in that a homeowners association maintains the common areas and that you must pay your fair share of the maintenance costs.

Although town house ownership offers certain freedoms, the entire project will be organized under a homeowners association with its own regulations to which you will have to agree as part of the purchase.

THE DETACHED SINGLE-FAMILY HOME

You don't need to worry about what the folks in the apartment next door think about you; you only have to worry whether you are violating the local zoning codes by storing that elephant you always wanted or whether the local noise ordinance was implemented after you moved in because your teenager has tried to rearrange his personal molecular structure by playing his stereo on the highest setting. You can paint the outside any color you choose, set up your Halloween and holiday decorations any way you want, and occasionally irritate your neighbor by mowing your lawn on Sunday morning.

Be aware that in the western states, large numbers of single-family detached homes are often clustered together in what are called **tract developments, clustered developments,** or **planned unit developments (PUDs)**. The building lots are small in size (an average of 60 feet by 100 feet), but the homes are spacious. Homeowners associations similar to those of condominiums are set up in most tract developments to maintain common areas.

HOW BIG SHOULD MY HOME BE?

All homes are measured in size by **square footage**. A square foot is just that, a square measuring twelve inches on each side.

Condos and co-ops are sized by the *interior square footage of living space* when advertised for sale, because they are incorporated into a larger project or building. Town houses and detached single-family homes are sized by the *overall square footage.*

To calculate the overall square footage (and thereby the cost of construction), a builder must measure the exterior dimensions of the entire structure. Measuring the overall square footage, however, does not give you the size of the living space of the home; the overall square footage includes the thickness of the exterior and interior walls. If you see a home advertised as being 2,000 square feet in size (the house size does not include the size of the land the house sits on), you must inquire whether this is living space or overall square footage.

If that number reflects the overall square footage, you can estimate that the thickness of all exterior and interior walls will take up approximately 100 to 200 square feet, depending on the style of home. If the advertisement indicates 2,000 square feet of living space, the home will actually be larger, but verify the description of the size with the seller or agent.

The easiest way to determine the overall square footage of a home is to measure the length and then multiply that figure by the width. If the home has two floors, then double your calculation. This does not include any attached structures.

The house in Figure 2-1 is 26 feet wide and 40 feet long. Multiply 26 times 40 and you get 1,040 square feet for the first floor.

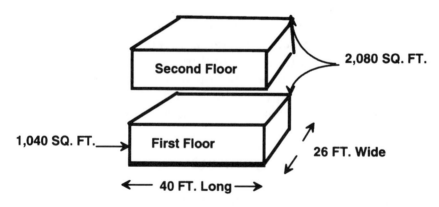

Figure 2-1.   Overall square footage.

Because this is a two-story home, it has 2,080 square feet of *overall square footage.*

Living space includes the living room, kitchen, dining room, bathrooms, hallways, closets, and any other area within the home that has been made into living space, including a family room in the attic or basement. Living space does not include a garage, carport, unfinished basement, or unfinished attic. Most advertisements for homes will quote the overall square footage of a home and also mention attic, full basement, or garage space. Occasionally, advertisers will quote the overall square footage of a home to entice a buyer to call when in fact the living space is much smaller.

HOW MANY ROOMS DO I NEED?

Needs versus Wants

One easy way to get an idea of how much room you need is to use the home in which you presently live as a guide. If your family is growing, you will need more bedrooms than you have now. You will also need more bathrooms and much more closet space. The dining room should be big enough to accommodate not only your immediate family but also your in-laws and friends.

The kitchen will have to be larger to accommodate all of those people, and a family room would be great for the kids as they grow. How about a garage with a workshop, a laundry room, and a big basement for additional storage? How big is this house going to be anyway?

When we start thinking about buying a house, all kinds of ideas start marching through our minds about *what we want.* They may not have much to do with *what we need.* When I built my own home in 1979, I went crazy with it. I sat down to plan the house, and by the time I was finished many weeks later, I decided that I had better win the lottery if this house was to become a reality. The house was eventually finished with less square footage than originally planned but still decidedly over budget.

I am a true believer in the KISS theory: "Keep it simple, stupid!" I remind myself of that theory every day. When looking for a home, do yourself a favor and keep it simple! Practicing this theory will keep you within the realm of reality.

Perception

Size is a matter of perception. To obtain an idea of room size, measure a room in your present living area. Multiply its length by its width to obtain the square footage of living space in that room. Do the same thing in all of your rooms to get an idea of size. Decide whether you need additional space for those areas.

By practicing measuring the room sizes where you live, you will increase the accuracy of your perceptions. When you are looking at houses, you will have an idea of the size of the rooms you will need; when you talk to salespeople on the phone, you can ask about the various room sizes and be able to visualize just how big they really are from their description. I have received many calls from potential buyers who ask, "Is it large? Are the rooms big?" Size is a relative term when you are on the phone; what is big to me may not be big to you. If you practice measuring your present living space, it will be much easier to decide on which homes you wish to see in the future.

How many rooms you need depends on your present and future needs—and most of all, on how much you can afford. We all need a room to sleep, a room to eat, a bathroom, and a living room. What we want may be something else, and the almighty dollar rules here. Remember the KISS theory. Concentrate on what you need first and make a list of those items. Concentrate on what you want second and list those items as well.

Now that you have obtained an idea of your present room sizes and have an idea about what you need, let's figure out how much you can afford before you run out of the door.

3

WHAT CAN I AFFORD?

We have all done it; now it's your turn. It's time to crunch numbers. This is the most complicated part of the entire process, but it is by far the most important.

Many times over the years I have met with buyers who had an image of their dream home already set in their minds. They were out in the evenings or on weekends searching in areas that they thought would be the best in which to live and raise a family. However, if you don't take the time to verify your finances *before* you go looking, you may be setting yourself up for disappointment. Make sure you can afford to buy the home you are looking for in the area you prefer before you spend considerable time searching. Spend time with the following formulas to see how your own numbers will work out. Take your time—play with them. If you can grow up, graduate from high school or college, find a job, get married, and/or have children, you can do this. Once you are comfortable with your ability to qualify for the financing, you become the **prequalified buyer**, the all-powerful American consumer. The sales professionals will not treat you like a mere looker, and your needs will be taken seriously.

The question is, can you not only qualify for a mortgage but also afford one? It may be that you have sufficient income to meet a lending institution's criteria for approval, but your lifestyle might keep you from being able to afford the monthly payments. To be sure of what's financially feasible for you, go through your records of your expenses for the past twelve months and fill in the blanks in the budget outline shown in Figure 3-1. Locate your W-2 tax forms from your employer for the previous year and check the amount of (combined, if applicable) gross income you received.

If some of your expenses are paid annually, divide them by 12 to break them into monthly expenses. Add all of your monthly expenses together to obtain your average total monthly living expenses. Subtract that amount from your gross monthly income, and the remainder is how much you can afford to pay for a mortgage. You may find that you will need to adjust your lifestyle to accommodate your mortgage payments.

Using the mortgage payment schedule in Table 3.1 can also help you to figure out how much of a mortgage you can afford. Simply slide your finger down to the interest rate you need and then slide again to the number of years you need to repay the mortgage. You will see a number known as a **constant number**, which represents the amount required to repay $1,000 for the number of years you chose at your chosen rate of interest. To find out how much your total monthly payment will be for your mortgage, multiply that constant number by your mortgage amount divided by 1,000. For example, if the interest rate is 9 percent and you need 30 years to repay the loan, the constant number is $8.05. If your mortgage is $100,000, multiply the constant of $8.05 by 100 (100,000 divided by 1,000), which equals $805. It will cost you $805 per month for 30 years, or 360 months, to repay a loan of $100,000 at 9 percent interest. Now try it yourself with your own mortgage amounts.

If the amount you come up with disappoints you, do not despair. In this chapter I will explain how you can choose a different type of financing, such as a lower-interest ARM mortgage. You can also use Figure 3-1 to help maximize your available income. Check the list for areas where you can cut down on expenses, such as work-related meals. If you average $10 per day for breakfast or lunch at work, you will spend at least $2,500 per year, which is more than $200 per month that could go toward your mortgage if you brought your food from home.

MONTHLY BUDGET OUTLINE FOR HOUSE PURCHASE

Gross Monthly Income = $	
Utilities	
Food for Home Use	
Clothing	
Car Payments	
Gas for Car(s)	
Insurance for Car(s)	
Auto Maintenance and Repairs	
Insurance (Life-Health) Premiums	
Personal Loan Repayments	
Credit Card Payments	
Work-Related Expenses (food, child care, commuting, dues)	
Medical Expenses	
Education Expenses	
Entertainment (movies, meals out, etc.)	
Personal Care (laundry, haircuts, beauty parlor)	
Magazine or Newspaper Subscriptions	
Vacation Expenses (if annual, divide by 12)	
Contributions to Places of Worship	
Home Maintenance: (cleaning, painting, lawncare, etc.)	
Club Memberships	
Total Monthly Living Expenses	

Figure 3-1. Budget outline.

Table 3.1. Mortgage Payment Schedule for Constant Level Payments Per $1,000

Interest Rates (%)	5 Years ($)	10 Years ($)	15 Years ($)	20 Years ($)	25 Years ($)	30 Years ($)
5	18.88	10.61	7.91	6.60	5.85	5.37
5.5	19.11	10.86	8.18	6.88	6.15	5.68
6	19.34	11.11	8.44	7.17	6.45	6.00
6.5	19.57	11.36	8.72	7.46	6.76	6.33
7	19.81	11.62	8.99	7.76	7.07	6.66
7.5	20.04	11.88	9.28	8.06	7.39	7.00
8	20.28	12.14	9.56	8.37	7.72	7.34
8.5	20.52	12.40	9.85	8.68	8.06	7.69
9	20.76	12.67	10.15	9.00	8.40	8.05
9.5	21.01	12.94	10.45	9.33	8.74	8.41
10	21.25	13.22	10.75	9.66	9.09	8.78
10.5	21.50	13.50	11.06	9.99	9.45	9.15
11	21.75	13.78	11.37	10.33	9.81	9.53
11.5	22.00	14.06	11.69	10.67	10.17	9.91
12	22.25	14.35	12.01	11.02	10.54	10.29
12.5	22.50	14.64	12.33	11.37	10.91	10.68
13	22.76	14.94	12.66	11.72	11.28	11.07
13.5	23.01	15.23	12.99	12.08	11.66	11.46
14	23.27	15.53	13.32	12.44	12.04	11.85

CLOSING COSTS

The size of your down payment will depend on the type of financing for which you qualify but will range from 3 percent to 20 percent of the purchase price. Settlement charges and closing costs can also vary from 5 percent to 10 percent of the purchase price, with an average of about 8 percent of the amount of the sale. The **closing costs** are for when you close title on the property; the **settlement costs** are the costs of the financing. Many brokers and lenders will quote the combined settlement and closing costs as one figure; make sure that you understand and receive a breakdown of costs for both sets of charges—just in case whomever you meet with only gives you one set of costs and not the other.

Most banks do not lend money for a residential mortgage that exceeds 80 percent of the appraised value of the property unless the amount that exceeds 80 percent is guaranteed by a federal program or private mortgage insurance (PMI). Conventional lenders that lend up to 95 percent loan-to-value require PMI insurance or Federal Housing Authority (FHA) guarantees to cover the amount that exceeds 80 percent of the loan. Veterans Administration (VA) loans do not require insurance.

I realize this all sounds complicated, but it will all come together as you continue. Practice with pencil and paper until you feel comfortable with the formulas in this chapter.

PRIVATE MORTGAGE INSURANCE (PMI)

Certain government-backed loans go as high as 97.5 percent of appraised value, but your qualifying ratio will be 29 percent of your gross income with no debts and 41 percent of gross income with debts. The **qualifying ratio** is the percentage of gross income used as a measure of your ability to pay normal living expenses and have enough left over for the mortgage. Loans approved for more than 80 percent loan-to-value and not insured by the FHA or VA will require private mortgage insurance, or PMI. FHA- and PMI-insured loans will require additional payments of premiums for this insurance. Currently the cost of private mortgage insurance is 0.0062 times the amount of the loan for the first year's premium and 0.00375 times the amount of the loan divided by 12 for the monthly premium (these formulas will vary).

The first year's premium is payable at the closing of the loan as part of the settlement costs. FHA-secured loans allow you to build the PMI premiums into the monthly mortgage payment. This premium is payable only when the balance of the loan falls below 75 percent of the **loan-to-value**, which is the percentage of the appraised value the lender will lend toward the property. At that time, you may contact the lender to have the PMI canceled. However, if your loan is sold to an investor group (the secondary market) as most mortgages are today, the new owners may not allow the PMI to be canceled. Many buyers forget to cancel the PMI, and the insurance companies reap the benefits with no liability to the lender.

You expected to pay closing costs, but if you need an insured loan, be prepared to pay the extra monthly insurance premium.

FHA AND VA LOANS

This is where the federal or state agencies become involved. I have already mentioned FHA or VA loans. Both of these agencies guarantee the repayment of loans made by private lenders using their own funds. For FHA loans, the government provides insurance against a default of the loan, with the premium paid by the borrower.

VA loans are guaranteed by the government and are available to qualified military veterans. The greatest advantage of these government-backed loans is the low down payment requirement, presently as low as 3 percent for qualified borrowers. Certain VA loans do not require any down payment at all, but the buyer must be qualified according to certain criteria.

State agencies may also have mortgage guarantee packages available. The State of New York Mortgage Agency (SONYMA) makes it possible for many to buy who otherwise would not qualify, but it sets income limits so that applicants will qualify for the lower-rate mortgage.

The mortgage calculations shown in Table 3.2 include a 20 percent cash down payment plus approximately 8 percent of the sale price for all closing costs. This would qualify as a standard conventional loan; however, the majority of loans approved do not require a 20 percent down payment. When you see how much cash you need, you can understand why the lenders invented other ways to finance mortgages. Most home buyers today, especially first-time buyers, simply do not have enough cash to cover such a down payment and still have enough left over to pay all the closing and settlement costs.

Do not be intimidated by Table 3.2. The majority of buyers do not have that much cash to play with. That is why you must understand the qualifying process and shop around for estimates. There are a wide variety of mortgage rates and an equally wide variety of mortgage types available. Many loans are designed to allow low down payments and even finance a portion of the settlement costs as part of the loan. Once you understand how to

Table 3.2.   Total Down Payment

Purchase price of home	$150,000.00
20% down payment required	−30,000.00
Mortgage amount	120,000.00
Estimated settlement costs (8%)	9,600.00
Cash needed to purchase and close title	$ 39,600.00

use the information in this and the next chapter, your goal will be much easier to reach.

HOW CAN I QUALIFY FOR THE MORTGAGE?

I've included an example in Tables 3.3 and 3.4 of the formulas currently used by most lenders and funding companies to prequalify their customers. I stress that these are just examples to help you understand the formulas used; just because you meet its criteria does *not* mean you are automatically qualified. Once you get a feel for what you can afford, you can then begin your search in the areas where you can afford to buy, thereby saving your time, other people's time, and your own peace of mind. Your new title will be **prequalified buyer**.

I strongly recommend that you call several banks and funding companies to allow them to prequalify you. The actual prequalification process involves more than just this formula. Your qualification status depends not only on income but also on the type of jobs you and your spouse have as well as your length of employment, job security, potential raises, credit history, and more.

Be careful of application fees. Most funding companies can give you an idea of what to expect without charging fees in advance. Ask whomever you call whether or not their firm charges advance fees, and if so, find a firm that does not.

Gross Income

There are many types of financing available today that allow buyers from a wide variety of income levels to find the financing they need to qualify for a mortgage. The most popular is the **30-**

year fixed-rate mortgage. Almost all banks and funding companies will first prequalify a buyer on the 30-year basis before placing that buyer in a program offering a different time frame. Use the examples in Tables 3.3 and 3.4 to prequalify yourself. This example is based on a fixed-rate mortgage for 30 years, or 360 months, at an interest rate of 8 percent. The buyer's gross income is $45,000 per year. Remember, gross income is all income derived from all sources, including part-time work (which must be verifiable for at least two consecutive-years), child support (which must continue for more than four years), inventions, or anything as long as the income qualifies.

Notice the difference between examples with no debts and those with debts in Tables 3.3 and 3.4.

Prequalifying with No Debts

Presently the qualifying ratios are 28 percent and 36 percent of gross income for conventional loans and 29 percent and 41 percent for loans above 95 percent of loan-to-value. These ratios may change; call the lender and find out what the current ratios are before you begin.

With no debts, $45,000 divided by 12 months equals $3,750 of gross monthly income. A lender will qualify you at 28 percent of gross monthly income if you do not have any other debts and at 36 percent if you have debts. Installment debts, such as credit card balances, are counted if they extend for more than ten months, which would include a car loan or student loan. You may be able to pay off a current debt and qualify with no debts if this formula meets your needs. Remember, if you are opting for a 95 percent or greater loan, your qualifying ratios will be 29 percent of gross income with no debts and 41 percent of gross income with debts.

Table 3.3 shows a formula for a buyer with no personal debts. She can afford to spend $790 per month toward the principal and interest of a mortgage. As you can see in the example, expenses for property taxes and insurance have already been subtracted from the gross monthly income. You have already been introduced to the term *PITI*, which stands for principal, interest, taxes, and insurance. To qualify, your gross monthly income must be such that you can pay 28 percent of it toward PITI if you have no other debts that extend over ten months or 36 percent if you do.

Table 3.3. Prequalification Formula with No Debts

Gross monthly income of $3,750.00 × 28% =	$1,050.00
Estimated monthly property taxes	−225.00
Estimated monthly insurance	−35.00
Net monthly income available for principal and interest	$ 790.00

Let's see how much of a mortgage this buyer gets with a principal and interest payment of $790 per month. By using the monthly mortgage payment schedule in Table 3.1 (page 18), once you have established your personal budget allowed for principal and interest, you can "back into" the mortgage amount for which you qualify.

Turn to the monthly mortgage payment schedule in Table 3.1 (page 18). At the top of the page, slide your finger over to the 30-year column. Now slide your finger down to the 8 percent line. You will see the constant number of 7.34, which represents $7.34 required to repay $1,000 at 8 percent interest for 30 years. If you need a $105,000 mortgage, multiply $7.34 times 105 to total $770.70. If you know how much of a mortgage you will need, play with the schedule by changing the interest rates 1 percent up or down or by changing the years required to see how you reach your level of affordability. Remember, these examples only use money available for the mortgage payment. You must also have enough money to pay the property taxes and home insurance.

What Is a Constant?
Our buyer has $790 per month to spend. The $105,000 mortgage will cost $770.46 per month, so how much more of a mortgage will the extra $19.54 buy? Mortgage tables are calculated by using a number, called a **constant**, based on so many dollars per thousand. In the left-hand column of Table 3.1, under interest rates, slide down to the number 8%. Now slide your finger to the right until you are under 30 years. You will see the constant number of 7.34, which reflects the $7.34 per month needed to repay $1,000 at 8 percent over a 30-year period. Change $7.34 to the decimal fraction 0.00734 to reflect the dollars-per-thousand ratio we're using. To find out how much more the additional payment can buy at 8 percent for 30 years,

divide $19.54 by the constant of $7.34 (0.00734), and you'll find that she can add $2,662 to the $105,000 amount for a total mortgage of $107,662.

Working with Constants

Estimate how much money you have to spend on a mortgage and divide that number by the constant number you need to see how much of a mortgage your money will buy. As an example, let's say that you can spend $843 per month on a mortgage. The best rate you can get is 8 percent, and you want to borrow as much as possible and repay the loan over 30 years. We know the constant for this formula is $7.34 per $1,000. Change $7.34 to 0.00734, divide your monthly payment of $843 by this constant, and you discover that you can borrow about $114,850. Find out what the current interest rates are and use Table 3.1 to locate the applicable constant number. Play with the numbers until you are comfortable with them.

Remember to allow for payments toward your property taxes in the amount you have available. *Most lenders require that your property tax payments be included with your mortgage payment.* The bank assumes the responsibility for paying the taxes to guarantee they will be paid. If you have $843 available and your estimated property taxes are $100 per month, you really have only $743 per month for the mortgage. Divide $743 by 0.00734, and you'll see that you now qualify for a mortgage of $102,624.

Add the estimated amount of cash required for the down payment and closing costs—about 8 percent of the sale price—and you have *the range of affordability.* For example, if you are buying a house for $120,000, you will need $9,600 to close title ($120,000 × 0.08 = $9,600).

Wait a minute, am I for real? Did I say that you will need about 8 percent of the sale price for the closing costs *plus* the down payment *plus* the costs of moving? Do you have hot dogs and beans available? Now you know why we all stock up on those items before buying a house.

If you do not have the cash available, don't be disappointed. A variety of mortgage programs will allow low down payments and even finance a portion of the closing costs, and although it sounds much too expensive, you will be surprised how many programs there are for buyers with limited cash. Cash gifts from blood relatives are also allowed.

Not too complicated, was it? You can see why I recommend performing a little arithmetic before you start your search. Once you become familiar with how these formulas work, you can narrow your search to the area and price range that fits your budget.

Prequalifying with Debts

Now let's consider a buyer with debts, like most of us today, using the same gross income. This buyer with debts qualifies to use the 36 percent formula (see Table 3.4).

Although Table 3.4 shows that $890 is available because the formula uses 36 percent of gross income, the lender will still use 28 percent of gross income to qualify the buyer for the principal and interest for the mortgage. The additional 8 percent (or any amount over the 28 percent requirement) must be used to reduce any debts. Most of us have other debts to pay, so to help you to qualify for the initial mortgage, the lender uses a higher qualifying ratio with the proviso that certain or all other debts will be paid off within a certain time.

This buyer has $890 available, and she wants a 30-year mortgage at 8 percent interest. If we divide $890 by the constant of 0.00734, we know this buyer can afford a mortgage of $121,253 if her gross income qualifies for that amount. Add $100 per month to the mortgage payment to account for a car loan, divide again by the constant of 0.00734, and you will see that for an additional payment of $100 per month, she can borrow an additional

Table 3.4.   Prequalification Formula with Debts

Gross monthly income of $3,750.00 × 36% =	$1,350.00
Any monthly expenses	−200.00
Estimated property taxes	−225.00
Estimated insurance	−35.00
Amount available for monthly principal and interest	$ 890.00

$13,624. For an additional $25 a month, she can borrow another $3,405. Play with the numbers until you reach your level of affordability. That may make the difference between buying your first-choice home or settling for a less expensive one.

Please keep in mind that this is only one example. There are many types of mortgages available with a mind-boggling variety of interest rates and payment plans. I will cover several forms of mortgages in the next chapter.

Also, please do not look up the adjustable rate mortgages (ARMs), which are less than the going rates for the 30-year fixed-rate loans; use the formulas above; and get all excited that you can now afford that mansion in the country you've always wanted. The lender will still qualify you at the current 30-year fixed rate of interest or at least at 2 percent above the current adjustable rates, even though you will start out at a much lower rate. The lender must look ahead with the possibility that your rate will adjust upward in the future. The lender will allow your qualification using a lower interest rate if the loan-to-value of the mortgage is less than 80 percent of the purchase price, thus making the loan less of a risk.

Percentages versus Fractions

It really gets interesting when you start to play with percentages of percentages such as 7⅝ percent or 6⅜ percent. The easiest way to end the confusion is to refer to Table 3.1 and find the dollars-per-thousand figures you need. Make sure that you look under the correct interest rate and the correct number of years.

If you really need to play with the fractions, then change them to decimal fractions as shown in Table 3.5.

Table 3.5.   Fractions to Decimal Fractions

1/4	0.25
3/8	0.375
1/2	0.50
5/8	0.625
3/4	0.75
7/8	0.875

As you see, an interest rate of 6⅝ percent is the same as 6.625 percent. Now you think it will be easier to figure out, right? Read on.

Add-on Interest

If mortgages were calculated by using an add-on interest formula, they would be easier to figure out, but you would end up paying much more interest than if the calculations were for the declining balance of the mortgage. For add-on interest, you start with the amount borrowed, multiply by the interest rate, add the two numbers together, and divide by the number of months needed to repay the loan. Table 3.6 shows the calculations for a loan of $100,000 at 8 percent interest with a repayment schedule of ten years using add-on interest. It is a simple way to calculate interest; however, it is anything but economical for a buyer.

Self-Liquidating or Declining-Balance Mortgages

Real estate mortgages are much more complicated than the example shown in Table 3.5. Almost all residential mortgages are written as **self-liquidating** or **declining-balance mortgages**. This simply means that part of your mortgage payment reduces the principal of the original loan and part reduces the interest. In the early years of the mortgage, the majority of the payment will be for interest. As you continue to make the payments, the interest is calculated monthly on the remaining principal, so the amount of the payment attributed to principal grows as the interest declines. (Obviously, add-on interest is far more costly.) This re-

Table 3.6. Monthly Payment Calculation with Add-on Interest

Amount borrowed	$100,000.00
Multiplied by 8% annual interest	$8,000.00
Loan period	10 years (120 months)
∴ Total interest	$80,000.00
∴ Total amount due	$180,000.00
Divided by 120 months of loan period	$1,500.00

duction of principal is called **amortizing** the loan. You will amortize the loan over the life of the loan, which is the length of time the loan is outstanding. Amortizing allows the principal amount of the loan to decline with each payment. The interest is charged only on the principal balance remaining; thus, the overall interest is less than what it would be if you used the add-on interest method. The amortized loan has a declining balance, which makes it self-liquidating.

Lenders have designed these mortgages this way not to take advantage of their customers but to maintain a profit margin on the average loan while at the same time making the loan affordable. The average buyer today will stay in his home about five to seven years before selling and moving out or up. Because the lender is committing the loan for a considerably longer time, most of its investment return must be recouped in the early years of the loan.

A good source of currently available mortgage rates is the real estate section of the Sunday newspapers. If you do not have a newspaper that publishes this information, contact your local banks. Notice that I used the plural! Banks are competitive and charge different rates; do not be afraid to call a number of them.

Please keep in mind as you crunch your numbers that these formulas **do not** indicate final qualification for a mortgage. I strongly recommend that you visit several lenders to get a better idea what your qualifications are. You will have a good idea of your level of affordability by practicing the formulas in this chapter. Use the practice sheet shown in Figure 3-2 to see how the formulas come together and practice using different interest rates and mortgage payment schedules, such as 15-year versus 30-year.

Once you have a feel for your range of affordability, you will save precious time by concentrating your search in the price range that meets your needs and fits your budget.

Note: When purchasing in a master planned community or a planned unit development, remember that these "clustered" communities usually form homeowners associations (HOAs) to take care of such things as outside maintenance and trash collection. Additionally, if your development requires a special improvement, such as a main road leading directly to a major highway, it may form a special improvement district (SID) for this purpose. You may be charged monthly fees by the HOA and/or the SID. The lender will take these fees into account when calcu-

PRACTICE MORTGAGE QUALIFYING WORKSHEET

GROSS ANNUAL INCOME DIVIDED BY 12 = GROSS MONTHLY INCOME.
BASIC QUALIFYING RATIOS ARE 28% WITH NO DEBTS AND 36%
WITH DEBTS.

PMI = private mortgage insurance; Home-Ins = homeowners insurance;
P & I = principal and interest of the loan

28% of Gross Monthly Income	36% of Gross Monthly Income
$_____	$_____
	$_____ Debt
$_____ Taxes	$_____ Taxes
$_____ Home-Ins	$_____ Home-Ins
$_____ PMI	$_____ PMI
$_____ P&I	$_____ P&I

Calculation for Monthly Payments

	Annual	Monthly
Taxes	_____	_____
Home-Ins	_____	_____
PMI	_____	_____
Totals	_____	_____
Add Debts	_____	_____

*Remember, the monthly PMI is calculated at 0.0037 times
the amount of the loan divided by 12. (Example: $100,000 × 0.0037 =
$370.00/12 = $30.83)

Figure 3-2.   Mortgage worksheet.

lating your mortgage amount, and they will affect the amount of mortgage you will qualify for.

WHERE DO I LOOK?

You will see many types of loan rates advertised by a wide variety of companies specializing in residential mortgages, predominantly banks, mortgage brokers, and mortgage bankers. Commercial banks will normally lend on a short-term basis for auto loans or business loans and have entered the residential mortgage market in a competitive way in recent years. The other types of banks are savings and loans and mutual savings banks, also known as thrifts. The thrift institutions specialize in residential home mortgages. Banks and mortgage bankers are also known as lenders.

Mortgage Bankers and Mortgage Brokers

Although banks offer many types of loans, they offer only loans that are approved by their board of directors, making them competitive but somewhat limited. **Mortgage brokers** and **mortgage bankers** are independent companies with contacts for a wide variety of loan types that they can place with a wide variety of lenders, including private lenders.

A mortgage broker will process the loan application and place it with a lender or mortgage banker. Mortgage brokers cannot approve loans or commit funds. Mortgage bankers may be more flexible in approving a loan because they can work with private sources of funds as well as bank money. I strongly suggest that you contact more than one and do not pay an application fee unless you decide to go ahead with that company.

Make an appointment with a loan officer to review your financial situation. He or she can make recommendations to guide you toward your goal. Ask the loan officer to provide you with a good-faith estimate of closing costs at each appointment to be able to compare costs.

Mortgage brokers and mortgage bankers are the wave of the future. They represent many sources of financing, and they continue shopping the markets to find the most competitive rates right up to the day the loan application is submitted. Remember to ask if the interest rate can be locked in if rates are currently climbing and how much the lock-in fee will be if any is charged at all.

The Interview

During the interview, the loan officer will ask you questions regarding your income, expenses, credit history, type and length of employment, and so on.

If you have had credit problems in the past, do not be afraid to speak up. In this age of supercomputers, credit cards, social security numbers, pin numbers, account numbers, phone numbers, ATM numbers, and the myriad of other distinguishing numbers assigned to us, whatever information you might try to hide from the loan officer will come out anyway. It is easier to determine the problem in advance and formulate a plan to correct it than it is to start the process over.

You will be asked about your combined gross income (assuming you're part of a couple), any debts that will extend for more than ten months, number and age of children, how long you've had your respective jobs, availability of cash, other assets such as stocks or bonds, value of life insurance, credit history, and more.

The lender simply needs to know three things—can you and will you pay the money back, is the property worth the price, and how much is too much to lend against the property?

Ask the loan officer if he or she will give you a copy of the application, a good-faith estimate (often called a **summary of costs**), and a copy of the fee schedule (see page 39) for you to take home and review. Remember, this is just an interview; unless you have already found a house and are ready to make an application for a mortgage, you don't need to sign anything or pay any fees. Put the information from each appointment in a separate envelope so as to be able to compare them later.

What Are Points?

With the preliminary information in hand, the loan officer will be able to give you a good indication of your qualifications for a loan and a general idea of how much you can expect to qualify for.

Along with all the other costs in the summary, you may see a heading for "discount points" or just "points." **Points** are considered as prepaid interest, payable in advance, and are fully tax deductible for first-time home buyers in the year of the purchase. For repeat home buyers and refinance customers, the points are tax deductible over the life of the loan.

A point is equal to 1 percent of the amount borrowed. You may be charged points as an origination fee and again as a loan discount fee. The **origination fee** is paid to originate the loan (and is a rip-off). The **loan discount fee** is prepaid interest to buy down the interest rate. As an example, if you borrow $100,000 and are charged 1 point, that 1 point is equal to $1,000. If you are charged 1 point as an origination fee and another point as a loan discount fee, you would be charged 2 points, or $2,000, for the $100,000 loan. If points are charged as a discount fee, write "prepaid interest" on your check before you hand it over. When tax time rolls around, there will be no question regarding the intended use of those funds.

When interest rates were fluctuating wildly in the late 1970s and early 1980s, lenders found it difficult to borrow money from the federal government and were short on money available to lend for mortgages. To solve this problem, **Fannie Mae** and **Freddie Mac** were created as secondary sources of investor money (see pages 54 and 55). These organizations are guaranteed by the federal government to provide huge amounts of money to lenders for home mortgages.

What Fannie Mae and Freddie Mac didn't anticipate were the enormous overhead costs required to shuffle those millions of tons of paper, and although the interest rate allowed the investors a good return on their investment, the cost of administering all of that money decreased the organizations' net profits. To combat this problem, customers were charged points, as additional prepaid interest, to cover the cost of administering the loan, thereby guaranteeing the investors the quoted interest rate as a return.

The lenders' year-end statements of profit and loss looked good because all of those points were shown as income for the year in which they were received, and the customers, slightly miffed at having to pay such huge fees, at least received their financing and deducted the prepaid interest from their taxes.

The mortgage market is subject to the whims of supply and demand just like the stock market and the real estate market. When money is plentiful, it is easier and less expensive to obtain, and the reverse applies when the demand is high.

In today's market, with rates back down in the single digits and the economy slowly inching along, fewer lenders may be charging origination fees, although I have little doubt that will change when the market perks up.

Mortgage brokers and mortgage bankers make their profits from the advance fees charged and occasionally from a portion of the points paid either directly by you or as a refund from the lender with which you are placed. Mortgage brokers are essentially wholesalers of paper, and lenders compensate them with a fraction of the points charged. The mortgage business is a highly competitive game (just scan the mortgage section of your Sunday paper) with rates, points, and no-point deals flying all over the page.

Occasionally, points or fees can be negotiable with mortgage brokers or mortgage bankers. The mortgage business is high volume, and these agencies make their money in bits and pieces. Many bits and pieces add up to many dollars, and most agencies would rather give up 0.25 or 0.5 point to make 1 point overall. Give it a try—if a mortgage broker is asking for 2.5 points on the deal, offer to pay 1.5 points. If you can meet in the middle or receive any discount at all, you've saved some money and started honing your negotiating skills.

On a mortgage of $100,000, a 0.25 point equals $250 and 0.5 point equals $500, so it is worth a try. However, if people are standing in line to borrow money, the mortgage agent may not be inclined to be generous. Any points charged should be in line with similar charges from other lenders, be they banks or brokers.

Do not allow yourself to become intimidated by the technical jargon. It sounds complicated and it is complicated, and loan officers may use this language extensively to impress you with their knowledge. Once you are sufficiently humbled by the onslaught of gobbledygook, they expect you to quietly follow directions, fill out a myriad of gobbledygook forms, and write checks as they bustle around the room trying not to be pinned down to a specific answer.

When someone does that to me, I like to revert to my "country boy mode" (remember this tactic; we will use it again). I simply sit back, relax, and try my best to look totally confused. At some point, someone will notice me and ask if there is a problem. I look at them with raised eyebrows and wrinkled forehead and quietly say, "I don't understand, I'm just a country boy, and this is all happening much too fast." Once they resume breathing, if you need further explanation for *anything*, ask them to review that item again and again until you are comfortable with it. You are about to assume responsibility for the largest financial debt to which you will be exposed in your entire life, so you'd best be comfortable with it.

I do not mean to imply by this that country boys are slow thinkers; quite the contrary, I believe country boys coined the term *horse trading*. I am considered a country boy by my customers from New York City, and that's OK by me.

What Does *APR* Mean?

Rather than points or interest, what you should be really concerned about is the **annual percentage rate (APR)**. The annual percentage rate is the actual rate of interest that you will pay, which may not be the rate advertised when discount points are involved. If points are charged, the lender must add that prepaid interest to the amount of total interest quoted to show the actual APR of the loan.

As an example, if the loan amount is $100,000, the annual interest charged is 7⅝ percent (7.625 percent) payable over 30 years, and the lender is charging 2.5 points, the actual annual percentage rate will be 7.89 percent, not 7.625 percent. Ask the lender's representative what the APR is as well as what the interest rate is.

When you make your appointments, be courteous and on time. Loan officers usually work on a commission based on volume of business, and time will be short. Remember that you are relying on this person to find you the best deal for your mortgage.

Obtain as much information over the phone as you can, although certain lenders will refuse to give you any information unless you go to their offices where they have a chance to sell you something. If you are simply shopping around, explain that to the representative, and you will not need to dig out your old tax records. If you have narrowed down your choices, they will ask for supporting information at the first meeting.

Remember to ask in advance whether the mortgage agency requires an advance application fee. An application fee is not normally refundable, and sadly there are those who will take your money gladly whether you receive the financing or not. Most successful agencies do not require advance fees. They will be happy to accept your fee when you have decided to accept their services after you have been prequalified.

Actual Annual Percentage Rate When Discount Points Are Charged

Review the schedule for points and discounts shown in Table 3.7. Along the top you will see the number of points to be de-

Table 3.7. Effective Interest Rates Where Discount Points Are Taken on a 30-Year Loan

Interest Rate (%)	1 Point (%)	1.5 Points (%)	2 Points (%)	2.5 Points (%)	3 Points (%)
5.00	5.09	5.13	5.18	5.22	5.27
5.50	5.59	5.64	5.68	5.73	5.78
6.00	6.09	6.14	6.19	6.24	6.29
6.50	6.60	6.65	6.70	6.75	6.80
7.00	7.10	7.15	7.20	7.25	7.30
7.50	7.60	7.66	7.71	7.76	7.81
8.00	8.11	8.16	8.21	8.27	8.32
8.50	8.61	8.67	8.72	8.78	8.83
9.00	9.11	9.17	9.23	9.29	9.34
9.50	9.62	9.68	9.73	9.79	9.86
10.00	10.12	10.18	10.24	10.30	10.37
10.50	10.62	10.69	10.75	10.81	10.88
11.00	11.13	11.19	11.26	11.32	11.39
11.50	11.63	11.17	11.76	11.83	11.90
12.00	12.13	12.20	12.27	12.34	12.41

ducted. In the column at the far left, you see numbers that represent the interest rate. In the columns to the right of the interest rate, you see the annual percentage rate (APR), or actual interest after points are charged.

As an example, move down to the first number (5) in the column under "Interest Rate." Now slide over to the right to the next number (5.09). Look above that number and you will see "1 Point." This means that if the interest rate quoted was 5 percent and the lender is charging 1 point, the APR is 5.09 percent. Even though you pay the points in cash in advance or finance them as part of your settlement costs, by law the lender must calculate those points into the overall interest costs of the loan to show the quoted interest plus the points to equal the total interest charged or the APR. The APR will change depending on the interest charged, the points charged, and the length of the mortgage.

Find out what the APR is for your loan before you commit to the transaction to verify that you are not paying too much overall interest for the loan.

Rate Locks

In today's volatile financial markets, interest rates change every day. The rate you see advertised or quoted by a lender will change tomorrow unless you are able to lock the rate for a specific time frame to gain your approval and close the loan.

When you meet with the loan officer and find a mortgage program with an interest rate that is acceptable to you, ask the loan officer if that rate can be locked. If it can be, ask for how long and at what cost. Nothing is free in the mortgage game, but you need to protect yourself from rate increases. Otherwise, you may find that by the time your application has been processed, the rates will have changed to the point that you will no longer qualify. If interest rates are falling and it appears that they will fall further, consider taking your chances and accepting a lower rate upon commitment from the lender. If rates are climbing and it appears they will continue to climb, lock the rate.

Interest rates are historically lower in the springtime because lenders are flush with cash and eager to get that money on the street earning a profit. Toward the end of the year, when most of the allotted funds are used up, rates will begin to climb—again, the old law of supply and demand. In addition to these laws, the Federal Reserve must keep an eye on the inflation rate. If inflation threatens to climb, it will raise the long-term interest rates as a protective measure.

Most mortgage rates can be locked for 30, 60, 90, or even 120 days. The lender will usually charge you a **lock-in fee** that may range from 0.25 point to a full point or more depending on the mortgage program for which you have applied. The lock-in fee will not be tax deductible since it is not considered as discount points or prepaid interest. Certain lenders require a rate lock for all loans, but many lenders do not charge a lock-in fee at all. Ask the loan officer if a lock-in fee is required.

The normal time frame to make an application and receive approval from a lender is four to six weeks (30 days in the Southwest). Once you receive the commitment from the lender, several more weeks will pass before you actually close title on the house. What good is a 30-day rate lock? It is good for the lender, which will be glad to charge you another lock fee. If you are going to lock the rate, lock it for at least 60 days and preferably 90 days in the event that Murphy's Law prevails and the sale takes longer to be completed than you had thought.

To close this chapter, I've included some practical examples that will help you understand what you're getting into. Figure 3-3 shows how settlement charges are calculated, Figure 3-4 shows how to calculate the application fees, and Figure 3-5 gives you a list of items you may need when you apply for your mortgage.

$_____ Contract Price

$_____ Mortgage Amount

$_____ Down Payment

$_____ Closing Costs

$_____ Cash Required (including per diem; see "Interest charges" below)

Listed below is the good-faith estimate of settlement charges made pursuant to the requirements of the Real Estate Settlement Procedures Act (RESPA). These figures are only estimates; the actual settlement charges may differ.

$_____ Loan Origination Fee (primarily for insured loans)

$_____ Loan Discount Fee (discount points)

$_____ Appraisal Fee (will vary depending on location)

$_____ Credit Report Fee (will vary depending on location)

$_____ Interest Charges (per diem, i.e., charged daily until the following month)

$_____ Mortgage Insurance Premium (PMI)

$_____ Attorney's Fees (lender's legal fees)

$_____ Title Insurance (not including fee policy; averages about 6% of the loan)

$_____ Recording Fees (to record the mortgage, note, and deed with the county)

$_____ Survey (costs to have the property surveyed if no survey is available)

$_____ Pest Inspection (becoming a mandatory requirement of most lenders)

$_____ Tax Escrow and Adjustments (Lender may require that at least one year's taxes be prepaid into an escrow account; the adjustments are the amount of taxes already paid by the seller that you must reimburse to them.)

$_____ State Mortgage Tax (if your state charges this tax)

$_____ Homeowners Insurance (Lender may require 1 year paid in advance.)

$_____ Buyer's Attorney Fee (if you use one or escrow company fee)

$_____ Fuel Adjustment (awarded to seller if fuel is left in the tank, if at all)

$_____ Water Test (if one was performed)

$_____ Well and Septic Certification (if one was performed)

$_____ RES Tax (service fee to update tax information)

$_____ VA Fee (for VA if applicable; usually 1.25 to 1.75 points)

$_____ Application Fee (fee paid to lender or broker for the application)

$_____ Other (if there are any)

Figure 3-3.   Example of good-faith estimate of settlement charges.

$_____ Application Fee

$_____ Credit Report Fee

$_____ Business Credit Report Fee (if self-employed)

Appraisal Fee Schedule (charged by the appraiser to inspect the home and offer a fair market value to the lender)

$_____ One unit

$_____ Two units

$_____ Three units

$_____ Four units

$_____ Co-op

$_____ Property Value (Ask for a quotation regarding your target purchase price.)

$_____ Final Inspection Fee (These fees are charged if the approval process takes longer than normal and the appraiser must return and do another inspection to recertify the original appraisal.)

$_____ Recertification Fee

Figure 3-4.   Typical application fee schedule.

Check off each item on this list, put it into a file folder, and don't lose it!

_____ Copy of an executed (fully signed) sales contract of the subject property

_____ Copy of the recorded deed (only for refinancing)

_____ Copy of executed (fully signed) sales contract of current residence (if you are selling)

_____ Copies of current year-to-date pay stubs

_____ Signed IRS 1040 forms with all schedules and W-2s for the last two years

_____ Year-to-date profit and loss statement signed by an accountant (if self-employed)

_____ Signed partnership tax returns with all schedules for the last two years (if you own 25% or more of a partnership; if you own less, you will need the K-1s)

_____ Signed corporate tax returns for two years (if you are an owner)

_____ College transcript or diploma if employed for less than two years

_____ Complete work history for the last two years

_____ Copy of executed (fully signed) lease if rental property is involved

_____ Gift letter (A gift of money from a blood relative is OK, but it has to be submitted to the lender as a gift, not a loan.)

_____ Proof of funds for a gift, i.e., a bank statement or letter from a bank on company letterhead

_____ Credit explanation of any known late payments or judgments

_____ Copy of separation or divorce agreements

_____ Proof of receipt of alimony or child support payments if claimed as income

_____ Copies of canceled checks or bank statement as verification of money for down payment

_____ Copies of stocks or bonds to be used for down payment or closing with proof of sale documentation included

_____ Copies of last 12 months' canceled checks or receipts for mortgage payments or rent payments

_____ Copies of your last 2 months' bank statements for all accounts

_____ Plans and construction specs if for new construction

_____ Copies of profit and loss statements on company letterhead for the last four years if self-employed

Figure 3-5.   Checklist of items you may need when you apply for a mortgage.

4

WHAT IS A MORTGAGE?

You are probably eager to get out there and begin your search—but finish your homework first. The more you understand the process and terminology, the easier it will be for you to complete your task successfully.

Let's begin this chapter by defining some terms. The term **mortgage** is derived from two French words, *mort* (dead) and *gage* (pledge), and dates back to the times of the Anglo-Saxons. A mortgage is a pledge to repay a loan using real estate as **collateral**, which is something of value given as security for a loan. The borrower is called the **mortgagor (obligor)**, and the lender is called the **mortgagee (obligee)**. The mortgage will be filed as a **lien**, which is a hold or claim that someone has on the real property of another. At the closing, you will sign a **mortgage note**, which signifies your responsibility to repay the amount borrowed. There will also be a **mortgage bond**, in which you promise to repay the loan on the terms agreed to in the mortgage note. The loan is amortized by repaying the principal amount of the loan over time. Loans that do not need a repayment guarantee by the FHA or the VA are called **conventional loans**.

Do not expect to remember all the terms mentioned in this book. To cover all the lending instruments and programs available would take another entire volume. I have concentrated on the most popular types of mortgages used today and given explanations of a few of the other forms used.

This book is a reference guide; take it with you throughout the process and refer to it as your needs arise. Refer to the index in the back of this book to locate the terminology you will be exposed to. Do not be afraid to stop someone in the middle of a conversation to look up the meaning of a word or phrase. Professional people just love to dazzle you with footwork and ten-dollar words. My feelings are that if you do not understand, ask for an explanation. If you do not receive a satisfactory explanation, explain that if you are not comfortable with the terminology and the process, you will go somewhere else.

WHAT IS AN APPRAISAL?

An **appraisal** is a means to arrive at an estimate of **fair market value** for a property, as defined by an appraiser, as of a specific time and for a specific purpose. An **appraiser** is a professional trained to verify the fair market value of property using several different formulas.

When money is plentiful, lenders need to get the money on the street quickly to earn their profits. At these times you will find it a little easier to qualify for the financing, and appraisers will be a little more lenient when appraising the value of property. However, when money is tight or the local market is in a decline, lenders become more conservative about the customers' qualifications, and the appraisers, hired by the lender (and paid by you), will have a tendency to be more conservative. Although you are charged for the appraisal, **the appraiser works for the lender, who is a repeat customer.**

Depending on the local market, if the appraisal for the home you want comes in substantially lower than that for comparable homes, feel free to question that appraisal and possibly demand that another one be performed by someone else. Find out why the appraiser felt that your desired home's value was so low. Point out the positive attributes of the house, such as better windows, better construction, or a better heating system. Most appraisers do not know that a cast-iron heating system is better than a steel-case system, but it is. If the appraiser will not back off and everyone thinks the appraisal is out of line, demand your money back, including the appraisal fee, and try another lender.

The appraiser must determine the value of the land separately from the structure to be able to place a value on the entire property. If the building is in disrepair but the condition and location of the land is desirable, the overall value should be more than that for a similar building in a less desirable area.

The appraiser will also consider the highest and best use for the property according to the uses allowed in the local zoning code and the actual design of the building. If the zoning allows multifamily as well as single-family use, the property should be more valuable due to the potential for more income in the future. However, although the property may be zoned for additional uses, the building design or floor plan must be able to accommodate the additional use without major renovation.

A typical appraisal should include the following items:

- The appraiser's qualifications
- Information on the general area
- A map of the area highlighting important attributes
- Information on the neighborhood
- A description of the scope of the appraisal
- Explanation of the purpose of the appraisal
- A definition of market value
- Description of the zoning that affects the property
- A copy of the zoning map
- A description of the property
- Plans or a sketch of the building(s)
- Pictures of the property and the surrounding area
- A copy of a flood plain map (if the property is located within a flood plain)
- A map or survey of the subject property
- Explanation of the highest and best use for the subject property
- Description of the method of the appraisal

- Description of the market, cost, and income approaches used to determine value
- A direct sales approach to the area and the land
- Comparable maps or surveys attributed to land sales
- For income property, a vacancy, credit loss, and expense analysis

Single-family and multifamily housing is the easiest to appraise because there is usually a constant flow of sales that continually update the market values and provide the appraiser with current information.

If the appraiser is based in a more expensive area and he or she is appraising property in a less expensive area, he or she may produce an appraised value that is higher than what local appraisers would produce for the same property. Local appraisers are more familiar with local markets. To gain a better understanding of such differences in perception, refer to the cartoon in Figure 4-1, which was conceived by my wife Carolyn and drawn by my son Marc. The sketch in the top left corner is the way that you see the house, the top right sketch shows how the seller perceives the house, the middle left sketch shows the lender's perception of it, the middle right sketch portrays the appraiser's point of view—and finally, the tax assessor's opinion is shown at the bottom. As you pass through the maze of home buying, you may feel that this is more than just a whimsical cartoon.

Because the lender will never see the property, it relies on the information provided by the appraiser. You can check with your sales agent to make sure that he or she provides the appraiser with every detail that could enhance the property's value. The appraiser will use the following methods to determine fair market value.

The Market-Data Approach

The **market-data**, or **comparison**, approach, which compares the subject property with other similar properties, is the most popular method of establishing fair market value. You will hear the real estate broker mention "comps," which is short for comparables. **Comparables** are similar properties used by the broker and

Figure 4.1.   Appraisal Cartoon.

the appraiser to establish the property's appraised value. As an example, if the home you are interested in has three bedrooms and two bathrooms, the appraiser will have to find comps that have sold in the same general area of the town or county with the same number of bedrooms and bathrooms. The same holds true for the condition of the home and the building lot.

If your target home has a family room, attached garage, or fireplace, the appraiser must find comps as close to your home as possible and make adjustments to the value to achieve a fair market value for the property.

The Cost Approach

Another method that appraisers use is the **cost approach**, which involves calculating the present-day cost of material and labor to reproduce the same structure at present-day costs. Most appraisers use the market-data approach and the cost approach when dealing with residential loans. They ask the real estate broker for comparables of other homes previously sold in the general area. Once the appraiser has established the value, the bank can determine the loan-to-value, or how much to lend against the **appraised value**. The appraiser must also consider the current market conditions. If the supply is high and the demand is low, the appraiser may have to cushion the appraisal with a lower fair market value, with the understanding that market conditions may force home values down in the future and the lender's mortgage may exceed its desired loan-to-value.

The Income Approach

An additional way to establish value is to use the **income approach**, which is reserved for properties that either produce income or have the potential to do so. The appraiser requires a breakdown of the existing or potential income and expenses as well as how the space is to be used. After combining all the other information compiled and including a risk factor for loss of income or increased taxes or insurance, the appraiser determines the additional value for the use and income.

HOW DOES A MORTGAGE WORK?

Fixed-Rate Mortgages

The most popular form of mortgage has been the **fixed-rate mortgage**. This means that the amount borrowed is charged a fixed rate of interest that will not change for the life of the loan. The monthly payment stays the same, although as time passes, your payment will include more of the principal and less of the interest, making the loan a declining-balance or self-liquidating mortgage (see Table 4.1). The standard for this type of loan has been a loan-to-value of up to 80 percent of the sale price or appraised value, whichever is lower. The lender will accept the appraised value over the sale price as the correct value for the property.

Adjustable-Rate Mortgages (ARMs)

Adjustable-rate mortgages (ARMs) are just that, adjustable. With the wild fluctuations in interest rates in the late 1970s, lenders realized that when they hold fixed-rate mortgages over a long period of time, they are subject to increases in the cost of money they themselves borrow or the amounts they must pay their depositors on CDs and other instruments. The banks found themselves paying out more interest than they earned. The ARM was born to combat that problem. The lender sets the rate for the first year, and the interest may go up or down at preestablished intervals ranging from three months to five years, with the most popular ARM adjusting annually depending on which index the lender uses to establish the rate. The index could be the yield for one, three, or five-year Treasury securities. Ask the loan officer which index will be used for your mortgage, how it has performed in the past, and where you can obtain annual copies. With an annually adjusted ARM, the rate adjusts on the **anniversary** of the loan—a year to the day you closed on the loan. Ask about the amount of the margin used to calculate the interest for your loan. The **margin** is the amount that the lender adds to the index rate to arrive at the interest rate charged on your loan. The margin amount remains constant, but the index rate changes every year. If you know the margin amount, you can combine it with the index rate to arrive at the totally adjusted rate.

If you do not plan to own the house for a long time, the ARM is more beneficial than a fixed-rate mortgage. The ARM will start out at a lower rate than the fixed-rate mortgage, with an annual cap on the increase. If you expect to own the house for a few years, you will save more by paying less interest in the early years than by paying the higher fixed rate from the beginning. Remember, the average owner today remains in his or her home between five and seven years. If you are unsure, ask the lender to provide you with a printout of an APR schedule that shows the actual interest rate charged for both the ARM and the fixed-rate mortgage and estimate the time you plan to stay in the home. Most of the monthly payment in the early years of both mortgages is interest anyway.

Loan Caps

Adjustable-rate mortgages place a cap on the amount that a loan's interest can increase per year; an overall cap for the life of the loan is known as a **lifetime cap**. If your loan starts out at 4.5 percent interest with an **annual cap**, that annual cap may be 2 percent of the original loan amount. This means the interest can rise to 6.5 percent after the first year and rise again 2 percent per year thereafter. However, before you panic, most states have implemented **usury laws** that allow the lender to increase the interest only to a certain point. The present lifetime cap for ARMs is 6 percent over the life of the loan, at 2 percent per year for a maximum of 10.5 percent. At today's rates, 10.5 percent is expensive; however, because the going rate is around 8 percent for a fixed-rate mortgage, the longer the economy allows lower rates, the more you will benefit by saving 2.5 percent in the early years of the loan. Even if the rate climbs to 6.5 percent next year, the fixed-rate mortgages are also climbing, and you will still be better off. Also, during that time you will have gained the tax benefits of ownership.

Another cap rate used is the periodical rate, which limits rate increases from one adjustment period to the next. If you have a periodical rate with an annual ARM (adjusted once per year) and an annual cap of 2 percent and the index climbs to 4 percent, then you will only be charged the cap of 2 percent for that year. Adjustable rates can decrease as well as increase as the index fluctuates. However, if the index remains at 4 percent for the following year, your rate will adjust upward another 2 percent.

Convertible ARMs

Certain ARMs, known as **convertible ARMs**, allow you to lock on to a fixed rate at a certain time if rates start to climb. Check with your mortgage professionals to see what the current options are. The fixed-rate mortgage and the ARM are the two most common mortgage instruments used today. Remember that the lender will still qualify you at the current fixed rate or at least 2 percent above the current ARM rate of interest, even though you are applying for an ARM.

Interest-Saving Loans

If you want to know more about other available options, you can ask about **interest-saving** or **15-year** loans. Taking out a 15-year rather than 30-year mortgage for $107,600 would save you $99,140 in interest. You save substantial amounts of money by reducing the number of payments (see page 56).

If you are able to repay the loan at a faster rate, do it. If you are unsure, stick with a 30-year schedule, get the mortgage, buy the house, and try to make additional payments toward the principal every year to quickly reduce the loan. You will be reducing your interest costs as well as building equity in the property much more quickly than you would if you simply stuck to the regular payment schedule. Even though the interest you pay may result in a tax deduction for you, the payment is still interest, not principal.

Variable-Rate Mortgages (VRMs)

The **variable-rate mortgage (VRM)** is not to be confused with the ARM. With a variable-rate mortgage, the interest rate is usually adjusted on a 6-month basis with a lower annual cap and a lower lifetime cap. The interest-rate cap is lower because the lender can adjust the rate every 6 months instead of every 12 months, which lowers the risk to the lender.

I will mention other types of mortgages just to make you aware of them. Ask the loan officer about the pros and cons of using these instruments.

Graduated-Payment Mortgages (GPMs)

The **graduated-payment mortgage (GPM)** is also a fixed-rate mortgage but differs in that the principal payment rises during the early years of the loan (the interest rate remains the same) according to a preset schedule. The payments start out lower and rise to a higher level in the middle or later years of the loan.

This loan is geared to younger purchasers whose income is expected to increase. Unless you are sure that your income will rise in the future, stay with the fixed-rate mortgage or ARM.

Growing-Equity Mortgages (GEMs)

Another mortgage designed to save interest by accelerating the payment schedule is the **growing-equity mortgage (GEM)**. This loan, unlike the GPM or ARM, is designed to reduce the principal amount of the loan by increasing the number (instead of the amount) of payments. A **biweekly mortgage** accomplishes the same task by reducing the principal in half the time. Again, unless you are positive that your income will increase in the future, stay with the tried and true.

Assumable Mortgages

You will also hear about **assumable mortgages**. Most ARM mortgages are assumable. Owing to the adjustable interest rate, the lender is taking less of a risk with rising interest rates and will allow the loan to be assumed by another buyer. The mortgage is already existing on the property, and you are able to assume (take over) the existing loan without having to pay all the closing fees for a new mortgage. When you assume a loan, you have to pay the difference between the purchase price and the balance remaining on the mortgage in cash. If the loan is not that old, you may be able to do it with less cash. If the loan is several years old, you might find it hard to come up with the cash required. If you are able to assume a mortgage, discuss the terms and conditions of the loan with the lender and your attorney. You are taking over an agreement that someone else agreed to. Make sure that you understand your obligations concerning the assumption. The lender may charge you an assumption or transfer fee to pay for the paperwork and filing fees.

Purchase-Money (Owner-Held) Mortgages

The **owner-held mortgage** is another form of financing. Instead of asking a lender to hold the mortgage, you ask the owner of the property to do so. You may find this opportunity when the market is very slow or interest rates are very high, forcing a slowdown in the market. The owner has had the property on the market longer than he would like, he has no other mortgage against the property, and he is eager to sell. If you can persuade the owner to hold the mortgage, you will avoid many of the settlement costs, such as those for the bank attorney and points. You will also find that the owner will charge less interest then the typical lender. This type of mortgage is also referred to as a **purchase-money mortgage**. The amount, interest, and terms of repayment are whatever you both can agree on. You will not have to go through the approval process; however, the owner should request verification of the same information that the bank would require. **Owner-held** mortgages are difficult to negotiate owing to the owner's need for money to move and pay off his own mortgage.

First Mortgages

All bank mortgages will be **first mortgages (primary loans)** unless the lender is financing another type of loan, such as a home-equity (secondary) loan. The bank will always be first in the event you decide to seek financing from other private or public sources for additional money using the house as collateral. Be careful if you do decide to obtain additional mortgages or liens against the property. Most mortgages require the immediate repayment in full of the entire balance due if additional financing is placed against the property without the written permission of the first mortgagee.

Second Mortgages

If you are short on cash and long on income, you may be able to persuade the owner to hold a **second mortgage**, which is also a lien on the property and enjoys the same rights as other mortgages. The second mortgage (also called a **secondary loan** or **wrap-around loan**) is just that, second in place behind a first mortgage.

The danger of a second mortgage is that in the event you default on the first mortgage and the bank forecloses, the second mortgagee will not be guaranteed its money in full. The bank holding the first mortgage will be satisfied first. What is left over can be paid to the holder of the second mortgage. Most sellers will not hold a second mortgage.

Balloon Mortgages

You will hear the term **balloon mortgage** or just **balloon**. As an example, a mortgage may be written to be amortized on a 30-year schedule, but the principal balance remaining may become due and payable (balloon) in the 15th year. A balloon is used by a lender to limit the risk to the lender of a lengthy commitment and to make the loan affordable at the same time by allowing the loan to be repaid (amortized) on a longer repayment basis.

Reverse-Annuity Mortgages (RAMs)

Another form of mortgage is the **reverse annuity mortgage (RAM)**, in which the lender pays the property owner a set amount each month depending on the age of the recipient and the value of the home. The RAM is an experimental mortgage used by retired people with too little cash and too much equity.

Shared-Equity Mortgages (SEMs)

A mortgage that you will be interested in if you are a first-time buyer short on cash is the **shared-equity mortgage (SEM)**. Blood relatives can loan you the money you need to accomplish the purchase. You agree that they will share in the equity buildup in the property for a fixed number of years. In the future, you refinance or sell and pay them back their principal amount plus their share of the equity.

Bridge Loans

A **bridge loan** is not a mortgage; it's a personal loan. Let's say you are transferred to a new area by your employer. You find the home you like, but you are short on cash for a deposit or down payment because most of your money exists as equity in your existing home, which has not yet closed title. If you do not presently own a home, you may have something else of value, such as stocks or bonds, that can be posted as collateral. Using the equity in these assets, it is possible to obtain a bridge loan from the bank or funding company you are using for the new house to bridge the gap in your finances until your existing home is sold.

Two-Step Mortgages

Buyers are able to finance the two-step mortgage at the prevailing fixed rate of interest for five or seven years. In the last year, the interest rate is adjusted at a fixed percentage increase, as much as 6 percent all in that year. Like an ARM, this is an adjustable-rate mortgage; unlike an ARM, the interest is only adjusted once instead of annually. Once the adjustment is made, that rate remains for the balance of the mortgage term. This allows the lender to increase rates if the cost of money goes up in future years. If you are borrowing when the rates are down and you qualify for a fixed-rate mortgage, why bother with the risk of a rate adjustment? If you are borrowing when the rates are high, it is a good idea to have the ability to adjust downward in the future.

Foreclosure

To **foreclose** means to take away the right to redeem. In real estate financing, if you fail to live up to your obligation to repay the loan, the lender can proceed to foreclose your property.

When you mortgage a property, you agree to allow the mortgage note to be filed as a lien against the property. You will sign a mortgage bond (also known as a promissory note), thus agreeing to repay the mortgage.

If you fail to live up to the agreements, you will be **in default** of the loan, and the lender has the right to foreclose the lien against the property, take possession of the property, and resell to recoup its investment.

Bait and Switch

As you make your way through the mortgage rate jungle, you will see that the rates do not vary substantially from one lender to another. However, you will see rates quoted at a very low level. They seem almost too good to be true, and they probably are. Advertising is designed to make you respond, and when you respond to an ad, you give someone the opportunity to entice you to buy. Lenders and brokers will advertise a **teaser rate** that is lower than most other rates and get your attention. Like anything else in the world, there is no free ride in the finance business, and although the rate may be attractively low, read the fine print.

I recently read a teaser rate placed by a local savings bank for a one-year ARM mortgage with an interest rate of 3.75 percent, an APR of 6.31 percent, and a two percent cap per year with a 9.75 percent lifetime cap. The ad said "no hidden fees." At the bottom of the ad, I saw this fine print:

> Upon completion of the fifth year of the balloon mortgage, customer has the option to refinance or pay off the existing balance. Rates are scheduled to change weekly. ARM rate may change after consummation. Annual percentage rate *includes points* and does not include PMI.

The ad stated "no hidden fees," but in the main body of the ad there was no mention of how many points would be charged. I guess points are not considered a fee. Also, you just read in the above paragraph what a balloon mortgage does. The advertisement entices the customer to call for the attractive low rate, but to accept that rate is to accept a mortgage that will require payment in full in the fifth year of the loan. In addition, the rate is subject to increases of 2 percent per year up to 9.75 percent; as well, points are calculated into the loan, but the ad does not say how many points are needed to obtain that attractively low rate.

I call this type of advertising a **bait-and-switch** tactic. The lender entices you to stop by its office by advertising the low rate. Once the professionals there explain the terms and cost of the loan, you will be presented with many other financing packages they offer—and then they *gotcha*.

Don't be offended. You will see this bait-and-switch tactic used often throughout your journey to home ownership—it's all part of the game.

Prepayment Penalties

Another common practice to make loans more comfortable is not to charge a penalty (this practice may change in the future) if you decide to pay off the loan early. Why would a bank penalize me if I paid its money back? Lenders commit the funds for a specific time at a specific rate of return on the investment. It is common today for most lenders to sell the mortgage off to the **secondary mortgage market**, which consists of an organization of investors sponsored by the federal government called **Freddie Mac** (the Federal Home Loan Mortgage Corporation), whose stock is owned by the thrift industry. The mortgages are packaged and resold as securities on the stock market. Another federally sponsored organization is **Fannie Mae** (the Federal National Mortgage Association), which provides funds to primary lenders and guarantees securities backed by a portion of its mortgage portfolio.

Your lender makes its profit by collecting the fees and points at the beginning of the transaction and earns a maintenance fee to continue servicing the loan.

If you opt in the future to repay the loan before it is due, because the lender has sold off the loan and the investors who bought it expect a certain rate of return, you could be penalized. Make sure that your mortgage has no prepayment penalty clause.

MORTGAGE AMORTIZATION SCHEDULES

Refer to Tables 4.1 and 4.2 to become more familiar with how amortizing reduces the principal while the monthly payment stays the same. Table 4.1 depicts the first 12 months of a 30-year mortgage. The principal amount is $107,600, and the interest is 8 percent. The first column shows the monthly payments, the second column shows the principal balance remaining after each payment, and the third column shows the monthly payment (which stays the same). The fourth and fifth columns show how much of the payment goes toward the principal and the interest, respectively. The first payment has been accounted for; the next payment is number 1. The principal decreases, so the mortgage is self-liquidating. The total deductible interest in the first year is $8,575.51.

Review the mortgage payment schedule in Table 4.2 that shows the first 12 months of a 15-year mortgage. The principal amount and interest rate are the same, but notice that by increasing the monthly payment by $238.75 per month, you can repay this mortgage in one-half the time. Also, as you did with the 30-year schedule, check the interest payment. Although the total interest paid is very close to that of the 30-year schedule, the interest declines at a faster rate and the principal climbs (amortizes)

Table 4.1.   First Year of a 30-Year Mortgage Payment Schedule

Payment Number	Remaining Principal ($)	Monthly Payment ($)	Principal Payment ($)	Interest Payment ($)
1	107,527.80	789.93	72.20	717.33
2	107,455.12	789.93	72.68	716.85
3	107,381.96	789.93	73.16	716.37
4	107,308.31	789.93	73.65	715.88
5	107,234.17	789.93	74.14	715.39
6	107,159.53	789.93	74.64	714.89
7	107,084.40	789.93	75.13	714.40
8	107,008.76	789.93	75.63	713.90
9	106,932.62	789.93	76.14	713.39
10	106,855.97	789.93	76.65	712.88
11	106,778.81	789.93	77.16	712.37

Table 4.2.   First Year of a 15-Year Mortgage Payment Schedule

Payment Number	Remaining Principal ($)	Monthly Payment ($)	Principal Payment ($)	Interest Payment ($)
1	107,289.05	1,028.28	310.95	717.33
2	106,976.03	1,028.28	313.02	715.26
3	106,660.92	1,028.28	315.11	713.17
4	106,343.70	1,028.28	317.21	711.07
5	106,024.38	1,028.28	319.32	708.96
6	105,702.93	1,028.28	321.45	706.83
7	105,379.34	1,028.28	323.59	704.69
8	105,053.59	1,028.28	325.75	702.53
9	104,725.67	1,028.28	327.92	700.36
10	104,395.55	1,028.28	330.11	698.17
11	104,063.24	1,028.28	332.31	695.97

at a faster rate even though the interest deductions are very close in the early years of the mortgage. The first payment was accounted for.

The following list sets forth various federal regulations to which you will be exposed that affect real estate and the lending practices related to real estate. They will apply to your purchase, loan application, and mortgage.

FEDERAL REGULATIONS REGARDING HOUSING
AND MORTGAGING

- ### Americans with Disabilities Act (1990)

  Requires owners and tenants of "places of public accommodation" to modify practices that discriminate against the disabled, provide auxiliary aids to communication, and remove architectural barriers (if removal can be readily achieved). Some examples are installing ramps, curb cuts in sidewalks and entrances, and raised toilet seats. U.S. Attorney General.

- ### Community Reinvestment Act (1977)

  Requires financial institution regulators to encourage banks under their supervision to meet the credit needs of their communities, including low- and middle-income neighborhoods and scrutinizes a lender's inner-city credit activities. Federal Reserve System, Federal Deposit Insurance Corporation, Comptroller of Currency, Federal Home Loan Bank Board, and Department of Housing and Urban Development.

- ### Consumer Credit Protection Act (1960)

  Requires accurate credit reports; allows consumers to correct inaccurate information in their reports; requires that credit reports be kept confidential, allowing access to properly authorized parties only; ensures meaningful disclosure of credit terms, allowing the consumer to compare other available credit terms to avoid uninformed use of credit; and protects against inaccurate and unfair credit billing and credit practices. Federal Deposit Insurance Corporation.

- ### Equal Credit Opportunity Act (1974) [Amendment (1976)]

  Requires financial institutions and other firms engaged in the extension of credit to make all credit equally available to all creditworthy customers without regard to sex or marital status. Compliance standards to prohibit discrimination are regulated by credit standards and loan application procedures prescribed by the board of governors of the Federal Reserve System. The 1976 amendment prohibits discrimination in lending on the basis of age, color, race, religion, national origin, or receipt by the applicant of public assistance. A lender must notify a prospective buyer within 30 days of application and if requested by the applicant, a reason for denial of the loan must be given. Steady part-time earning must be considered by the lender in evaluating a loan application. Federal Home Loan Bank Board, Comptroller of

Currency, Federal Deposit Insurance Corporation, and Federal Reserve System.

- **Fair Housing Laws**

    Prohibit discrimination on the basis of minority status in the sale or rental of any house, apartment (or other residential structure), and vacant land; require that each client be treated as an individual and be served according to individual needs and desires. Department of Housing and Urban Development.

- **Home Mortgage Disclosure Act (1975)**

    Provides information to assist in determining whether depository institutions are serving the housing needs of their communities and neighborhoods; helps public officials determine the distribution of public sector investments in a manner designed to improve the private investment environment and contains a detailed reporting system. Federal Home Loan Bank Board, Comptroller of Currency, Federal Deposit Insurance Corporation, and Federal Reserve System.

- **Interstate Land Sales Full Disclosure Act (1968) [Amendments (1979)]**

    Requires developers of subdivisions with 25 lots or more to file a property report and a statement of record with the Office of Interstate Land Sales and with the secretary of the Department of Housing and Urban Development, prior to promoting or offering subdivided land for sale or lease; applies to land sold or leased in interstate commerce; recent revisions involve property reports and regulations for filing financial reports and advertising. Department of Housing and Urban Development.

- **Magnuson-Moss Warranty (Federal Trade Commission Improvement Act) (1975)**

    Establishes mandatory standards for warranties on consumer products to improve consumer information, prevent deception, and improve competition in the marketing of consumer products; requires a written warranty, as required by the rules of the Federal Trade Commission, to fully and conspicuously disclose, in simple language, the terms and conditions of the warranty; includes new home appliances and other equipment that are an integral part of plumbing and heating systems. (Wiring, piping, and other similar items are not covered; however, home builders are responsible for satisfying warranty claims concerning warranties they provide on these items.) Federal Trade Commission.

- **National Mobile-Home and Construction Safety Standards Act (1974)**

  Establishes federal standards for the construction, design, performance, and safety of mobile homes. Department of Housing and Urban Development.

- **Real Estate Settlement Procedures Act (RESPA) (1974) [Amendment (1975)]**

  Encourages homeownership by regulating certain lending practices as well as closing and settlement procedures in federally related mortgage transactions to minimize unnecessary costs and difficulties of home purchase; provides the prospective borrower an information booklet on the nature and costs of real estate settlement services when an application for a mortgage loan is made. (Booklets may be printed and distributed by lenders if form and content are approved by the secretary of the Department of Housing and Urban Development [HUD].) A 1975 amendment permits the HUD secretary to exempt certain localities, where settlement statements are not customarily provided, from the required uniform settlement statement and permits the statement to be modified for different parts of the United States. Federal Home Loan Bank Board, Department of Housing and Urban Development, Federal Deposit Insurance Corporation, and Comptroller of Currency.

- **Regulation B (Title VII, Consumer Credit Protection Act) (Amendments)**

  Requires lenders to notify potential borrowers of action taken on their loan applications and to provide a written report on adverse action or a written statement of the prospective borrower's right to receive this information; addresses the terms under which a creditor can and cannot deny credit. Federal Reserve System.

- **Regulation Z**

  Includes regulations pertaining to consumer credit disclosures issued by the board of governors of the Federal Reserve System pursuant to Title I (Truth in Lending Act) and Title V (General Provisions) of the Consumer Credit Protection Act (See **Truth in Lending**.) Federal Trade Commission.

- **Section 8 Program**

  Assists low- and moderate-income families in obtaining decent, newly constructed, and substantially rehabilitated housing, in accordance with provisions; promotes economically mixed housing;

includes a federal rent subsidy program for low- and moderate-income tenants and permits developers of new or substantially rehabilitated multifamily housing to contract for housing assistance payments on any or all units and be eligible for financing; was created by the Housing and Community Development Act of 1974. Department of Housing and Urban Development.

- **Truth in Lending Act (1968)**

  Ensures a meaningful disclosure of credit terms so that consumers know of the cost of credit and can more readily compare terms and avoid uninformed use of credit; promotes economic stabilization and strengthens competition among financial institutions and other firms that extend consumer credit. Federal Trade Commission, Federal Home Loan Bank Board, Comptroller of Currency, Federal Deposit Insurance Corporation, and Federal Reserve System.

- **Truth in Lending Simplification and Reform Act (1980)**

  Amends the Truth in Lending Act of 1968, making significant changes in credit disclosures that creditors must make to borrowers. (Information required by this act must be disclosed conspicuously, and the terms *annual percentage rate* and *finance charge* must be disclosed more conspicuously than any other terms, data, or information provided in connection with a transaction, except information relating to the identity of the creditor.) Federal Trade Commission, Federal Home Loan Bank Board, Comptroller of Currency, Federal Deposit Insurance Corporation, and Federal Reserve System.

- **Veterans Housing Benefits Act (1978)**

  Amends Title 38 of the U.S. Code to improve the housing benefits program of the Veterans Administration; provides for increased loan guarantee and direct loan amounts, authorizes the Veterans Administration to approve loans for home improvements involving installation of energy-conserving devices such as solar heating and cooling systems, and reduces the amount of time of service required for Vietnam veterans to be eligible for loans. Veterans Administration.

5

HOW CAN I FIND IT?

Now that you know more about what you need, what you can afford, and how to finance it, you need to concentrate your search in areas where you can afford to buy. Start by making a list of your present concerns, such as

- Commuting time and distance to work
- Type of car and gas consumption
- Existing size of family
- Future size of family
- Medical requirements of family
- Types of schools you prefer
- Availability of sports programs
- Availability of local shopping
- Road systems available
- Buses or trains available
- Places of worship

DRAW A CIRCLE

A driving time to work of one hour or more is not unusual today. Buy a map of your target state, pinpoint your present location, and decide how long a commute you can live with. Locate the mileage chart on the map, estimate the distance from your present job location as the starting point, and draw a circle completely around that point. For example, let's say that your map shows one inch to be equal to 25 miles. You feel that a commute of 50 miles is acceptable. Starting at your present or future job location, measure out two inches and draw the circle. This will show you all the areas that fall within 50 miles of your job.

Check the types of roads available, such as interstate highways, parkways, major routes, and secondary roads. Choose the most logical places to begin your search and visit them.

CHAMBERS OF COMMERCE

If you are moving to another state, contact the state, county, or town chambers of commerce before you make the trip. The chambers of commerce can provide you with such information as median income for the area, population counts, housing availability, and local industries. If your search is directed to a specific county, buy a map of that county. Using the state map as a guide, draw a circle on the county map that corresponds to the commuting distance you previously accepted. Within that new circle, you will see several areas to focus your search. Visit those areas and purchase local newspapers, pennysavers, or free publications. Take the time to read through these publications to get an idea of what housing types are available and their price range.

ASK QUESTIONS

Drive around using the county map and become familiar with the roads. Locate the shopping areas, hospitals, and business centers. Stop for coffee and ask the waitress about the housing market in the area, which school districts and towns are the most popular, which real estate brokers are the most popular, how high the taxes are, which industries are supporting the area, whether any new companies are moving in, and how the local water quality rates in comparison to that of other areas. Are there car pools for commuters, are there commuter trains, are there airports, where are the major hospitals? Ask as many questions as you can. Stop for gas and ask the attendant the same questions; when you buy the newspaper, ask the person behind the counter the same questions. Stop at a supermarket and check the food prices. Check the prices at a local dry cleaner. Write down as much information as you can about local costs of living to compare them with your present costs, especially if you are moving from state to state. If the cost of living is higher in the area you are moving into, check your budget amount for house payments. You may have to compromise the type of house or your existing lifestyle.

ASK MORE QUESTIONS

My wife Carolyn recently had a customer experience "sticker shock." She is moving to southern New York State from the Midwest with a substantial increase in wages to compensate for the added cost of living. She visited the location she was interested in and compared the cost of living, right down to including the cost of dry cleaning, with her present cost of living. She determined that even though she had been offered a substantial raise in salary to relocate, the cost of living at the new location was such that she would not see any savings from the move.

When you ask questions, you get answers—all kinds of answers—and armed with them, you will start to get an idea of what that area has to offer. Municipalities update the general information about their areas every several years. If your focus is on a specific town, contact the town hall for similar information and inquire about any local chambers of commerce that may exist there.

KEEP RECORDS

While you're driving, make notes on the map or on a separate paper regarding points of interest, shopping centers, schools, and so on. Follow the same procedure for every area you visit, and keep all the information about each area in a separate envelope.

When you get back home, review the information you have collected and make notes of your discussions. When you visit several areas in a short time, if you do not attempt to separate the information, you stand the chance of not remembering vital information and becoming confused.

I am a constant note taker. Whenever I have a business meeting with anyone, I bring a pad of paper and jot down portions of the conversation, especially important facts that affect the transaction. This practice has saved my bacon more than once over the years.

If a dispute develops, no matter what the reason, I can refer to my notes and avoid the "he-said, we-said" syndrome.

If you are viewing a particular home that has certain attractive items like built-in book cases or mirrored walls, do not assume that these items will remain with the home upon sale. Most often, something attractive purchased by the sellers will move with them.

Ask the sales agent or seller if these items are to remain and write down the answer. Better yet, ask the sales agent to write down—on her letterhead—all the attributes of the house that interested you and that the agent claimed added to the value of the home. Date the paper and ask the agent to sign it. If it turns out later that a mistake was made, you have it on paper.

HOW DO I QUALIFY THE LOCATION?

As you accumulate your information, you will be able to narrow down your search to a specific geographic area, possibly within a single town or an area that may encompass several towns. Concentrate within that area and ask more questions of everyone you meet. Qualify that area according to how well it meets your needs.

Visit Main Areas

Drive around the secondary (back) roads as well as the main routes. Visit the schools, hospitals, playgrounds, parks, shopping centers, places of worship, and the town hall. Drive through several communities, such as a village and all the new subdivisions. The style of homes and the price range in the new subdivisions will indicate the current market for new homes in the area.

Builders accumulate as much market information as they can before investing hundreds of thousands or millions of dollars in a new development. They will meet the demands of the strongest market to sell their homes quickly.

You must visit several sites to get an indication of the strongest market. If the builders are concentrating primarily on smaller homes or larger, custom homes, that is usually the current market.

For-Sale Signs

As you drive around, you will see for-sale signs placed either by the owner or a real estate broker. Write down the names and phone numbers on the signs in front of houses that interest you.

If you are interested in a particular home, locate it on your map and check the surrounding area for commuting routes, schools, shopping, and the like. If you wish to see the house, call to make an appointment (but first, review the next chapter to qualify the house). If you find a particular area attractive, don't be afraid to stop and ask questions of anyone you see in the immediate area, preferably someone who owns a home there. You will be amazed about how much inside information you can receive about an area by simply listening to the gossip. If the information is consistent among several people, it may be true.

FSBO

FSBO is an abbreviation of "for sale by owner." You will find it in newspaper ads placed by owners who wish to sell direct and save the brokerage commission. If you find a home you like through the owner, make sure that you write everything down to avoid any misunderstandings later. You do not have the third party (sales agent) there to verify any information given by the owner. The owner has only one house to sell and will understandably make the best sales pitch to entice you to buy. With a sales agent, you have the opportunity to look at a number of properties and obtain a perspective different from your own, thus enabling you to view the properties with a more objective eye.

If you find an FSBO home you want to buy, sit down with the owner with pen and paper and list all the terms and items that are included in the sale. Do not draw a contract. (I will cover contracts in chapter 12.) You will want to think about it and negotiate the price and terms over several days. If the owner wants a good-faith deposit to hold the property off the market until you can conclude the deal and you feel the opportunity warrants giving him a check, write on the check that it is a deposit only and is subject to the signing of a formal contract within two days. Postdate the check for three days later so that it cannot be cashed before a formal contract can be signed. In the eastern United States, most of this procedure is handled by an attorney; in the western states, you must handle it or hire an attorney; when using a broker, the agent draws the agreement. I do not recommend your signing agreements and writing checks unless you have a third party overseeing the transaction. Caution: in the western states the purchase offer *is* the formal contract; attorneys are not involved.

Sticker Shock

If you are moving from a rural area to a more metropolitan area, be prepared for housing prices to be higher. That beautiful colonial-style four-bedroom house you purchased in the Midwest for $65,000 will cost about $365,000 in Westchester County, New York. You may want to take the easy way out and simply start your search by calling local real estate brokers and letting them answer your questions. If you do, remember that the salesperson is interested in only one thing: to sell you real estate. I recommend that you find out as much about an area as you can before you contact a real estate agent. This way, you will have qualified the area yourself, focused on a specific area to search, and familiarized yourself with the local market conditions, and you will be ready to qualify the real estate agent.

HOW DO I QUALIFY THE REAL ESTATE AGENT?

Remember that one factor in the purchase of real estate is the art of compromise. We all compromise on the area, the street, the style, the color, the yard, the price, the terms, and other items. Even if you have your heart set on a particular style of home, be willing to compromise if you do not find exactly what you want.

It may or may not be out there, and are you willing to spend months or longer trying to find it? Remember, if demand is high and you are not willing to compromise, you may miss a chance at finding the best available home.

If you were referred to a particular agent by a friend or family, you are in good company. According to the 1991 study done by the National Association of Realtors, 80 percent of those surveyed purchased their home using the professional services of a licensed real estate broker, and 77 percent of those surveyed selected the broker through a referral from a friend. In the language of the real estate industry, you are known as a **principal purchaser**, and the seller is known as the **principal seller;** you will both be called the **principals** of the transaction. You have accumulated many titles in a short time.

You may see advertisements on local cable TV stations or in publications for specific homes for sale. The ads were placed either by the real estate company or by the listing agent herself. You will see advertisements that say "cute as a button," which may also mean "cute but small." Other favorite phrases, "handyman's special" or "needs TLC," usually mean "needs work." Such advertising is a way to entice you into the office so that the agency can present you with many opportunities. A prospective purchaser rarely buys the advertised house that prompted the call.

Listing versus Selling Agents

A **listing agent** is one who procures the listing of the property for the real estate company; a **selling agent** is one who sells the listed property. The listing agent has the most information regarding the property. If an agent sells a property that was listed by another agent, after the commission is shared with the real estate company, the listing and selling agent will share their portion of the sales commission using a separate formula. If the sales agent is also the listing-agent, he shares the commission only with the broker.

Agent Qualifications

In previous years, all you needed to obtain a state license to act as a sales agent was to find a licensed broker to act as your sponsor, study, and pass the test. When I first began my career in the business, a good many people with licenses only worked part-time while holding down another full-time job. Although many licensed agents still work part-time, a majority of those licensed today work on a full-time basis. In the 1970s most states adopted new laws governing real estate licensing requirements. To qualify for your license, you must now complete a minimum continuing education course of 45 hours. The course deals with the **principles and practices laws** of the state regarding real estate transactions, and most of those teaching the courses are either attorneys or qualified licensed brokers of long standing in the community.

In years past the licensed agent might have been the shoemaker or the shoemaker's wife who had no formal training in the business. Today you should find, with few exceptions, a highly motivated, educated, and professional group of people that still might include the shoemaker's wife.

What is a Realtor?

A **realtor** is a licensed **principal broker** (a licensed broker who is a principal of a brokerage firm) who is a member of his or her local, state, and National Association of Realtors (NAR). A **Realtor Associate** is a licensed salesperson or associate broker who belongs to the NAR. Many real estate agents today, especially if they are affiliated with a large office, belong to the NAR, which sets forth a Code of Ethics and Standards of Practice to establish standards for its constituent agents that are higher than those required by law. Having dealt with many real estate agents over the years, I have found that those agents who aspired to become NAR members handled their trade in a very professional manner. I do not mean to say that all of those licensed must be Realtors. To join the NAR is voluntary, and I have met many licensed agents throughout the years who were not members and did an equally professional job.

Fiduciary Responsibility

Historically, a licensed agent maintained a fiduciary responsibility to the seller to sell the property at the best price and terms acceptable to the seller. **Fiduciary** means "related to or of a confidence or trust"; thus, the agreement to use the services of the agent to sell the property was made in the trust that the agent would act in the best interests of the seller. In most states, that fiduciary responsibility was written into law.

In recent times, we have seen the emergence of buyers-brokers, which are agencies that offer a fiduciary alliance to the buyer instead of the seller. The agent must disclose for whom he or she is working.

Most real estate agents realize that although the law may require them to represent the seller (unless they have disclosed that they represent the buyer), if there is no sale, the entire procedure is redundant. Sales agents walk a very fine line between the interests of the seller and buyer and their own self-interest—which is to make the sale and earn their commission. No matter who represents whom, the main focus of the exercise is to sell and make money, and the art of compromise plays a major role in the outcome.

In the western states, where contracts are drawn by the brokers and closings are handled by escrow companies and attorneys play a minor role, the need for a buyer's representative is strong. In the eastern part of the country, where state laws are so prolific and representation by an attorney is almost a requirement, I question the need for a dual brokerage situation. The bottom line is, that you should do whatever makes you comfortable. The majority of sales agents are interested in selling you a home, making a commission, and accomplishing all this in a professional manner.

Disclosure

You will be asked to sign a **disclosure form** as an acknowledgment that you understand that the agent is working on behalf of you or the seller. At the initiative of the National Association of Realtors, 44 states now require mandatory disclosure of the agent's representation. In the recent past, if an agent had a buyer for a specific home listed by an agent associated with a different office, they would agree on a commission split and would agree to **cobroke** the listing. By law, both agents would work for the seller. It is perfectly legal for a licensed agent to represent the buyer, as long as the agent discloses to all parties her intention to do so.

A buyer's agent may ask that you pay a fee in advance for his representation because he may not be paid by the seller. Ask the buyer's agent if paying the requested fee will mean that he won't demand a portion of the commission if you buy. If the buyer's agent works both ways—demands a fee and a portion of the commission—then why pay the fee? If the buyer's agent accepts a fee as total compensation for his service, ask if his normal share of the commission is discounted from the sale price; if so, you may save a substantial sum. The only problem I have with the advance fee system is that because the agent has already been paid for services not yet performed, where is the incentive to find the best deal, where is the incentive to protect you, and where is the incentive to help make the transaction flow smoothly to its conclusion?

If the buyer's agent does not arrange in some way to be paid by you, he can also look to the seller for compensation, provided that the agent discloses to the seller that he is a buyer's broker working on behalf of the buyer. The seller must sign a disclosure form acknowledging the agent as a buyer's broker and agree to pay the commission to the broker if there is a sale.

You may have heard the phrase *caveat emptor* (Let the buyer beware), a term used in ancient England when farms were sold together with simple homes without all the heating, water, and electrical systems we see in the modern home. Today, the almighty consumer has gained significant influence through the courts. Most states are contemplating a requirement that the seller (and possibly the broker) sign a disclosure statement regarding any potential or existing defects in the home. Many licensed brokers have purchased errors and omissions insurance to protect them in the event a home has a major defect that was not uncovered or disclosed by the sales agent. The sales agent is required to disclose any information regarding any known defects to a potential purchaser. The brokers are now requiring the sellers to disclose the same information to them before listing the home.

A broker or agent must also disclose to the seller that she is a licensed sales agent in the event she intends to purchase the property for herself and to the buyer if she holds a personal interest in the property she is selling.

Be Courteous

The real estate business is a seven-days-per-week career. I have received phone calls for appointments on Christmas Day, during holiday meals, before six in the morning, and after eleven in the evening. I will tell you that I did not appreciate those calls, and I was not in the mood to be helpful to those inconsiderate enough to make them.

I advised you to be courteous and prompt toward the loan officer; the same holds true for the sales agent. The sales agent works hard to gain the education to maintain the license, works harder to research the market to gain the knowledge necessary to sell, works even harder to find good listings among potentially tens or hundreds of homes, and works harder still to advertise those listings in the right places to entice you to call.

Good agents will develop a network of other sales agents in other offices with other listings and buyers and develop another network of sources for financing and legal advice. While they are doing that, they will attend interoffice meetings to learn more about their own agency, attend other associated functions such as chamber of commerce meetings and seminars, attend functions performed by the local realtor associations, and more—all just to be ready when you call. For the most part, agents spend additional money for their own advertising and work strictly on a commission basis. In addition, they try to have a life with their own families.

I suppose by now you are thinking, boy, does this guy have a biased opinion about brokers? Yes, I do. Real estate has been my life and my family's life. I know what sales agents have to go through to reach that level of professionalism and to make a living. It is very hard work to be successful in any sales business, especially a sales business that involves such large amounts of money. I have found that if you show someone who is trying to help you the same courtesy that you would expect if the roles were reversed, then your experience will be a happy one.

The sales agent is looking for the house you described in the area you prefer and in the price range you established. You will probably ask the agent about sources of local financing, attorneys or escrow companies who deal mostly in real estate, where to get a good deal on appliances, and more. You will be relying on the agent to help you through the process quickly. If you are courteous and treat the agent as a professional, you will be satisfied with the service you need. A partner of mine who was much more successful than I, once mentioned to me when I was acting particularly arrogant that "an ounce of honey accomplishes more than a pound of vinegar." He was right.

Mention to the agent that you know other people (if you do) who are looking to buy homes in the same area. Sales agents hear this all the time and frankly, most of the time it doesn't work out that way. Sometimes it does, however, and agents would love to have a referred customer who didn't cost them advertising money. If you like the agent, mention her to everyone you know. We all know someone interested in buying real estate. You will build a strong working relationship and even a new friendship.

Qualify the Agency

When you call to inquire about the listing, feel free to ask about the real estate company itself. How many years has it been in the business, how many salespeople does it employ, and how many listings does it handle per year? Ask the same questions of the agent. If you ask, you gain knowledge.

To save time, explain to the agent that you have already been prequalified for a certain amount of financing (I hope by now that you have). A good agent will ask for this information in advance anyway to save time for both of you by showing you not only what you ask for but what you can afford to buy. Explain the price range you are interested in and the style of home you would prefer. Specify the number of bedrooms, bathrooms, finished playrooms, fireplaces, or any other features about the inside and outside of the home you would prefer. Remember what you decided that you need and what you want. Be ready to compromise, because the perfect home has yet to be built.

The Multiple Listing Service (MLS)

By giving the agent this information in advance, before setting an appointment, you allow the agent time to research the lists of existing homes for sale either through a multiple listing service or by calling other offices that may have something close to your needs. The **multiple listing service (MLS)** is a computerized list of all homes listed with the service and is broken down by area and price range. Allow the agent to call you back with a description of the various properties, and if appropriate, set up an appointment to visit those sites. If the agent simply invites you to come in and skim through the current **multiple listing book**, she is not doing her job. Your time is as valuable as the agent's, and she should be prepared to show you several homes within your price range that have at least some of the features you said you wanted.

The appointments should be made and a schedule set up before your arrival at the agent's office. Besides simple courtesy, another good reason to show up for your appointment on time is that the agent will set up a specific schedule for visiting the various homes with various sellers. You might find the home you like and have to deal with an irate seller who works the night shift and will not be happy to sit and wait. If you are going to be late, call the agent quickly to rearrange the schedule. The agent should also be knowledgeable about the general area, current financing trends, and current sale prices of similar homes.

Changing Agents

You are under no obligation to stay with one agent or one office. If you see an advertisement for a listing with another agency, feel free to call that agency and follow through with the same process. However, if you find an agent who is professional and works hard to satisfy your needs and with whom you are comfortable working, stay with that agent and have him investigate the other listings for you.

The danger in hopping from agent to agent is that you will see some of the same listings shown to you by the previous agent. This creates a problem for the agents in the event you decide to buy a property that was already presented to you by someone else.

To consider their commission truly earned, agents must prove that they were a deciding force of the sale. They must show the properties to you, present you with all pertinent information relating to the property, follow up with you on all properties presented, and actively pursue the sale to you.

If you decide to use another agent from a different office and the new agent presents you with properties you have already seen, inform the new agent that you have already seen the property with another agent and tell her who the agent was. If you offer to purchase the same property where two agents are involved, the sale may be jeopardized by more than one claim against the property for the commission. However, if you are not comfortable with the agent with whom you are working, inform him that you would prefer to shop around and if he finds anything to let you know. The real estate industry is just like any other industry; there are good people and not-so-good people. I have been exposed to both, and I'm delighted to inform you that, with a few exceptions, I have been satisfied with my dealings with various agents.

The Agent's Job

An agent's responsibility is not only to find that perfect house but also to keep in touch with you on a regular basis to see if your situation has changed or to notify you of any changes of which you should be aware. Professional agents will be able to narrow down the wide range of possibilities to a few homes that meet your criteria within a short time. If you are going out week after week looking at homes that you cannot afford or do not satisfy your needs, the agent has not paid attention and is wasting your time. If you find the agent to be too pushy or if she has a personality that makes you uncomfortable, don't burn any bridges; she might just find the house you need, but tell her you are going to continue to look around and find another agent with whom you do feel comfortable.

6

HOW DO I QUALIFY
THE HOUSE?

Assuming that you have accepted the geographic location, size, number of rooms, neighborhood, school district, and asking price from the information provided by the realtor, review the following paragraphs to inspect each home you visit. You do not have to perform a lengthy inspection at each home; I doubt that either you or the agent will have the time.

Ask the agent which items stay with the house as you go through each one. That Tiffany dining-room ceiling light that you fell in love with may not be part of the sale. If you don't ask as you go through the house, your opinion may be swayed by items you think will stay. If you like a particular home, ask the agent to show it to you again.

Tell the agent that you wish to do a thorough inspection and set the appointment to allow you enough time to satisfy yourself that the home meets your needs. Bring a camera and take pictures of each home you see that you would entertain buying. Attach each picture to the corresponding inspection checklist like the one at the end of this chapter, and you will be able to remember the various attributes related to each home.

Usually when you are out on appointments, you will exit the car and go into the house, but before you do that, take some time to check the grounds and the exterior of the home first. Subject to the age of the home, you have to pay attention to the things you can't see as much as the things you can see. Most resale homes, to enhance the sale and sometimes to hide defects, are freshly painted. Sometimes the sellers will install new carpet or vinyl flooring. Although these improvements improve the appearance of the building, they will not be able to hide important potential problems.

HOME INSPECTION SERVICES

There are many home inspection services that will give you a complete rundown of the condition of the property. You will normally not hire an inspector until you have negotiated the sale and signed a purchase offer (see chapter 14) for the house. Certain inspectors are former builders or real estate brokers, and others are either licensed engineers or professionally trained inspectors.

Ask whomever you contact if they are members of the National Institute of Building Inspectors (NIBI) or the American Society of Home Inspectors (ASHI). Both of these organizations offer training as well as a code of ethics and standards of practice, and both certify their members. I would lean toward the professionally trained inspectors or licensed engineers, especially if they carry **errors and omissions and liability insurance.** Errors and omissions insurance protects them in the event they fail to inform their client of a situation that becomes a problem after the sale. The insurance also protects you—if you can prove that the inspector made a mistake, the insurance company will pay to solve the problem.

I recommend that you hire a home inspector who does **only** home inspections, **not** inspections and repairs, just to avoid any potential conflict of interest. Ask the sales agent and your attorney for the names of several home inspection companies. You should call the inspector to qualify him and you should hire him, instead of allowing the agent to hire him. Sales agents are like water; they will always take the path of least resistance, and they build referral associations with various contractors over the years. There is nothing wrong with that, but the inspector knows that he will work for you only once, whereas he may be called by the agent many times.

Although most home inspection companies do a great job, I have experienced a few that, despite their licenses, presented the property in such a critical way that they frightened the buyers away when the problems were really not that severe. If you experience this problem, ask to meet with the inspector on site to have the problem explained to you. Once you understand the situation, if the solution is expensive and you really want the house, obtain a second opinion from a different inspector and then make your decision. If the problem is legitimate, obtain an estimate from the inspector for the cost of repair. I would be surprised if the seller is unaware of the problem, and he or she may be willing to negotiate the cost of repair from the purchase price.

INSPECT THE CONDO, CO-OP, OR TOWN HOUSE

Although you are buying the inside of a condo or co-op, you are also taking responsibility to pay your fair share of the outside maintenance and repair. With a town house, you are buying the *inside and outside* together with your fair share of the common areas' maintenance costs.

Sellers of large projects use many gimmicks to sell their product, especially if the project is several years old and has been converted from a rental to a sale property. If the project is several years old, you have to inspect the entire project to see if the roads, the siding, and the roofs are in good shape. How about the recreational areas like the pool and the clubhouse? If they are in need of repair, you will be paying for those repairs in the future.

One tactic used is the sale of an entire apartment project to a group of investors with the intent to convert the project from rentals to sales. The investors notify the existing tenants of the conversion and offer them rock-bottom deals to buy their own units. They give notice to the tenants who cannot or will not buy to move out after a specified time, and they spiff up the exterior of the project with new signs and paint—carefully avoiding spending money for major repairs. They cffer the balance of the job to the general public at very attractive prices and with special financing incentives to sell out as fast as possible.

The kicker is that although the new owners' monthly maintenance fees start out low, when the roofs leak and the boilers break down and the road needs to be fixed in the future because the project is old and the investors did not spend for needed repairs, they will start paying substantially higher monthly maintenance fees, which could climb higher than the mortgage payment if the repairs are extensive. How does that affect them? Not only are they spending much more for maintenance, but the resale value of that project will also be lower due to the excessive maintenance fees.

When looking at condos, co-ops, or town houses, be sure to ask about the projected costs for future maintenance. How old are the roofs, the heating systems, the water and sewer systems, and the laundry facilities? If they have never been replaced and the job is ten years old or more, watch out.

Items to pay particular attention to in multifamily housing are the water heater, sliding glass doors, windows, air conditioners and their wall sleeves, and the appliances. All of these items are prone to wearing out. The doors and windows are probably not the best quality and loosen over time, letting cold air inside. If the unit has electric heat and the complex is more than five years old, have an electrician inspect the baseboard heating units and the circuit breakers to verify they are in good working order. Again, builders of large projects tend to buy the least-expensive materials, and those materials will not hold up for the long haul.

Another feature to check is if the building has a fire wall installed. A **fire wall** is a wall that extends from the basement floor up through the roof. The wall can be made of concrete block or framed out and double-sided with firecode Sheetrock. However the wall is constructed, find out what the burn rating is for the wall. The **burn rating** is how long it will take for a fire to burn through the wall. The burn rating should be at least one hour and preferably more.

In older projects, fire walls were not a code requirement, and when one unit burned, many others burned with it. Fire codes were changed to require that a fire wall be installed at the end of each group of four living units, and the newer codes may require a fire wall at the end of each unit. Ask the project superintendent or the homeowners association if a fire wall exists and if so, what its burn rating is. If they don't know, contact the local fire inspector. The fire inspector has a copy of the plans for the project or will have inspected it and will know about the fire walls.

START FROM THE BOTTOM

On the outside, you start at the bottom with the foundation. In many areas of the southern and western states, houses are built **on slab** (also known as **slab on grade**) or with a crawl space, which means they do not have a full foundation under them.

One reason homes are built this way is that local ground conditions make the cost of a full foundation prohibitive. **Ground conditions** include the elevation of the land and whether there is clay, rock, gravel, water, or a mixture of any or all of these under the surface.

Where Does All the Water Go?

If the soil is mostly clay, water will not penetrate or be absorbed as quickly or at all. This promotes **surface drainage,** in which the water will run on top of the surface or just below the surface through the topsoil. In rocky conditions, such as those found in most areas of the western states, water can also run along the surface and create erosion problems because rocky soil has very little topsoil (humus) to hold a root system for grass. The surface conditions in the western states promote severe erosion caused by water runoff in many areas. Gravel soil is ideal, which means soil mixed with many small stones of a variety of sizes. Water can be better absorbed into the soil by flowing around those small stones.

Water under the surface, **ground water,** is a problem because unlike surface water, it doesn't drain away. **Surface water** includes water that runs along the surface of the ground (or just below the surface), penetrates up to several feet into the ground, and can be redirected to flow away from the house. Ground water is better described as water that has penetrated and accumulated more than several feet into the ground or that flows underground naturally, such as an underground spring. This ground water layer is called the **water table** (see Figure 6-1).

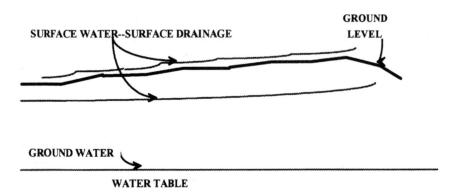

Figure 6-1.   Surface water and ground water.

In most areas, there is always water somewhere in the ground—it's just a matter of how far down you have to go to find it. In southeastern states such as Florida, the water table is very high; you can dig down a few feet and hit ground water. Certain areas will have a high water table, and other areas will not.

To build a full basement seven to ten feet into solid rock or high water is simply not practical. But you can build a full foundation into clay as long as you provide enough drainage to allow the surface water to drain away. You can accomplish this by grading the elevation of the ground around the house to promote drainage away from the foundation and by providing **footing drains** along the bottom of the foundation to allow any water against the foundation to flow away.

The measurement of the high and low points is called the **topography** or **topo.** Figure 6-2 shows a side view of a topography. The land depicted drops from a high point (100 feet elevation) to a low point (70 feet elevation), which is a drop of 30 feet. To determine the **percentage of grade,** you need to know how deep the property is. As an example, if the lot in Figure 6-2 is 300 feet deep (from front to back) and the elevation drops 30 feet, then divide the amount of drop by the depth: 30/300 = 10 percent grade.

A property can have many high points and low points, and you can calculate the various elevations (contours) by measuring how far each contour rises and falls by the width of the contour. If the contours are far apart on the map, the land is level; if the contours are closer together, the land is steep. In the 300-foot-deep lot in

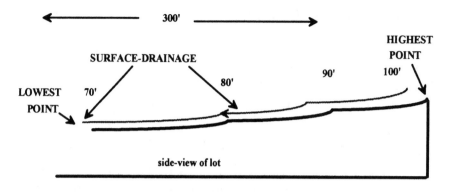

Figure 6-2.   Topography.

Figure 6-2, there are four contours, so the elevations are 75 feet apart: 300/4 = 75. Most topographical measurements on a survey map will be anywhere from 10 to 2 feet apart depending on the size of the property. A drop of 10 percent over a depth of 300 feet is not bad at all.

The **slab-up** style of construction (also known as slab-on-grade) is just that—the first floor sits at ground level and is made of a poured concrete slab. There is no basement, and the balance of the home is built from the ground up. The crawlspace style of construction includes a space several feet high between the slab base and the first floor, which is usually made of wood, and the balance of the home is built from there. In the Northeast and some parts of the Midwest and Southeast, buyers usually prefer to have a full basement to allow for more storage or future living space. Figure 6-3 illustrates these various designs.

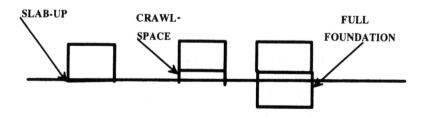

Figure 6-3.   Slab-up, crawlspace, and full-foundation designs.

LOOK BEFORE YOU LEAP

Before you enter the house, take some time to check the elevation (topography) of the building lot. Stand on the front of the lot—then near the edge of the road—and then about in the center of the lot. Face the house and see how the lot looks. Is it perfectly flat, higher in the front, higher in the back, or higher on the right or left? Does the house sit centered on the lot, or is it more to one side? Unless the lot is larger then the norm for the area, if the house is not centered on the lot, it was probably set there to accommodate the driveway or possibly an attached garage. The reason you should check the elevation is that when it rains or the snow melts, all of that water will be draining from the highest point on the lot to the lowest point. You can practice sighting an elevation by observing the area surrounding where you presently live.

Water may be the giver of life, but it is a major problem for homeowners if the lot's elevation does not allow it to drain away from the house. I cannot count the number of inquiries I receive on a regular basis from buyers searching for level lots. A level lot is great if the ground conditions are such that any water will be immediately absorbed into the soil. The problem arises when an early spring thaw or torrential rains melt the snow, causing the ground to become saturated. If you do not have an elevation on the lot that will allow water to drain away from the house, the water will pond and most likely end up **in** the house.

Check the surrounding area. Is the lot higher or lower than the surrounding area? Is there a hill across the street? Is the neighbors' lot higher than yours? Where does the water flow on the road when it rains, toward the lot or away from it?

Check out the landscaping for dead or diseased trees that may cause a problem in the future and for excessive shrubbery that blocks the sun, allowing areas of the house to remain damp and thus become perfect breeding grounds for mold.

YOU LEARN SOMETHING EVERY DAY

A few years ago I purchased a level lot. Soil tests indicated that the lot was mostly gravel. The engineering studies produced by the owner did not indicate any problems. I did not build on the lot immediately but held onto it for several years, waiting for the housing market to increase.

I went into a partnership with a friend, presold a house for the lot, and started construction in December of that year. We **stick-built,** which means that we constructed the home on site—piece by piece—instead of buying a factory-made (modular) house that is delivered in sections. Everything was fine until we were into the wet season with rain and snow. The water table rose considerably overnight, so much so that it covered the foundation. We couldn't understand why, because the lot was dry gravel, until we looked around the surrounding area within a one-mile radius and realized that almost all the surrounding countryside was higher than our lot.

When it rained or the snow melted, the ground water, or water table, for this lot would rise until the moisture stopped and then immediately lower. Although the lot was level, with gravelly soil, it had one flaw—the water table was seasonal, high during the rainy-season and low during the remainder of the year. All of our engineering and soil tests had been done during the dry season. We resolved the problem by installing a system of drain pipes under the basement floor with a pumping system to take the water away before it could enter the basement. If this problem had come up after the house had been sold, it would have been a real problem indeed. I learned something that day.

Figure 6-4 shows how the elevation of the surrounding area, even as far as five miles in any direction, can affect your lot.

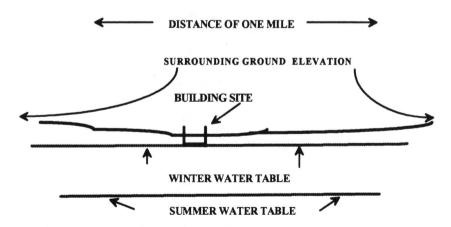

Figure 6-4.   Summer water table.

LOOK FOR WHAT IS NOT OBVIOUS

Inspect the area where the ground meets the foundation. Check for indications that water has been left standing or has created a flow pattern. Evidence of areas of standing water could indicate clay or rock under the surface. (Clay or rock can be found in pockets; they won't necessarily be found under the entire lot.)

Check for leaders (the drain pipes from the roof gutters to the ground) and gutters. One sure way to let water into the basement is to allow the water to run directly off the roof and thus land right next to the foundation. Check the foundation itself. Almost everything you are buying is sitting on it.

If you see an area of dampness or a formation of mold, it's a sure indication of consistent moisture that could be caused by water from the roof, or from the ground—or it could simply be an area that is never exposed to the sun and never thoroughly dries.

While you're inspecting the exterior grounds, look around the surrounding area as far as you can and then determine in which direction the house faces. In areas with cold winters, we need all the help we can get, and solar heat does make a difference. If there is a hill to the east of the house, the sun may not reach it until later in the day; if something is blocking the sun from the west, the afternoons will be shady. (Remember, the sun is higher in the sky in the summer and lower in the winter.) If the house is facing east, you will see the sun in the front of the house in the morning and in the rear of the house in the evening. If the house is facing south, you can benefit from solar heat almost all day.

In the Southwest, you'll want to be in the shade of a hill or mountain most of the day. In colder parts of the country, you'll want a good southern exposure for winter and shade trees to block the sun in the summer.

An abundance of glass is great for southern exposure in the winter, but if you do not seal that area from the cold at night with insulated drapes, you can lose all the heat you gained during the day. Most of the heat is lost through the windows and doors.

HOW DO I QUALIFY THE HOUSE'S CONDITION?

Foundation

If the house is old, has a stone foundation, and has been sitting there for decades, any problems with the foundation should have passed long ago unless the owner modified the construction. The most common types of foundations used today are concrete block and steel-reinforced poured concrete. The main advantage of concrete blocks is that if you want to modify the basement later, it's much easier to break apart or drill a hole in a block than to attempt to do so with steel-reinforced poured concrete. Although I feel that poured concrete will take more pressure than concrete blocks, it's more a matter of preference or cost than requirement.

The exterior of the foundation should be coated with a waterproofing material such as hot tar or liquid asphalt from the ground level down to the **footing,** or bottom of the foundation. Builders may use a masonry sealant and **parge,** or coat, the exposed foundation walls. I recommend both. Water is a builder's enemy and must be kept at bay. During periods of excessive rain—meaning heavy rain for at least several days—even in gravel soil, there can be as much as 1,500 pounds per square inch of water pressure against your foundation. If there is but a pinhole, water will find it.

It is normal for houses to settle for months or even years after construction. There is a tremendous amount of weight pressing down on the foundation. It is not unusual to see **settling cracks.** Even poured-concrete foundations experience some cracking due to settling or **curing** (drying) of the concrete as the moisture leaches out. If the settling cracks are in the mortar between the concrete blocks, there may not be a problem. If the cracks extend *through* the blocks, actually breaking them, this indicates a potentially serious problem.

Any crack that appears bigger than a hairline crack is a potential problem. It may be due to the house or ground shifting after construction or to a design flaw that causes too much weight to be concentrated in that area. Or it may be that the **footings** under the wall have cracked. If the footings have cracked, you will experience a chronic settling problem that normally cannot be resolved unless you jack up that part of the house, take out that portion of wall and footing, and replace it with new material that is married together with the remaining section of wall. Figure 6-5 shows the difference between a simple mortar crack and a wall crack caused by a broken footing.

If there has been a chronic settling problem, you will see areas where the wall has been continuously patched. You will also see

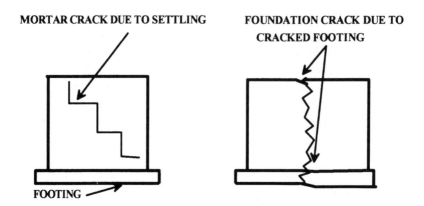

Figure 6-5.   Footings.

areas on the walls or ceilings inside the house where the settling has caused cracks in the plaster or Sheetrock. Another indication of a house shifting is when the doors or windows stick when you try to open them. Depending on the climate in the area, it is normal for a house to expand in the heat and contract in the cold. The house is built with those conditions in mind. If you are visiting the house in hot, humid weather, the doors or windows may stick owing to expansion of the entire house and thus of the door or window. In cooler weather, that condition will reverse itself.

One sure way to allow water into the foundation is to allow water to accumulate around it. If the house does not have gutters along the roof or leaders to drain the water from the roof and direct it away from the foundation, all of that water falls directly against the foundation. The ground will become saturated, and the water will pool in pockets underground and eventually find its way into the home.

Just the other day I went to my friends' home for dinner. They had recently rented the home, and as they were unfamiliar with home construction, they asked me to inspect an area in the basement playroom where the inside foundation wall showed dampness. I went outside to the area corresponding to the dampness and found a roof drain (leader) tied into another buried drain that was designed to carry the water from the roof and empty it several feet away from the house.

The metal of the roof drain had cracked in several places. My diagnosis was that the underground drain had become plugged, probably with leaves. The water draining from the roof had backed up, frozen, and expanded inside the leader, thus cracking it and allowing the water to drain freely against the foundation.

When the underground drain was dug up, it was in fact plugged with leaves. They bypassed the underground drain and installed an extension on the bottom of the leader several feet long to direct the drainage away from the house, and to date the problem has not recurred.

Not all problems have to have a complicated solution. Sometimes what first appears to be a major problem has a simple and inexpensive resolution. If you can recognize a simple problem that everyone else thinks is a major problem, you can negotiate the purchase price based on the "major" problem and save money by repairing the real, simple problem.

The Water Problem

As I explained in the above paragraph, sometimes what appears to be a major problem really isn't. I have experienced episodes throughout my career in which evidence of some type of moisture problem in a house causes the house to be automatically labeled as having a water problem.

I explained earlier about the difference between surface water and ground water. Surface water (which includes water draining from the roof) can be made to flow somewhere else; ground water must be dealt with on its own terms.

Obviously, if you visit a house with four feet of water in the basement, there is a water problem. If you visit a house that shows evidence of dampness, there is a problem also, but both of these conditions can be rectified. If you like the home, try to determine what is causing the problem, either on your own or by hiring a professional to guide you to a solution.

Don't automatically walk away from what may be your dream home because the house has been labeled as having a water problem unless you find the problem cannot be resolved to your satisfaction.

If there is a problem, most often the seller is well aware of it and may negotiate to help or even pay for a resolution to sell the house.

Siding

Check the siding for cracks, stains, bleaching by the sun, and loose sections. There are many types of sidings used today, such as cedar or redwood on upscale homes that are either stained with color or left natural, or sprayed-on masonry siding, which is used predominantly in the western states. The most popular siding in the east for midscale homes is vinyl siding. Aluminum siding was the most popular type in the 1960s owing to its ease of maintenance. Aluminum siding comes in a variety of colors and sizes, but those colors are painted and baked on and have a tendency to fade in the sun. Aluminum also has a tendency to dent when something is thrown against it, such as a stone or baseball. However, aluminum siding requires little maintenance and will hold a darker color.

New technology has all but removed those objections in recent years, but vinyl siding remains the most widely accepted in the east. Vinyl siding is economical and easy to apply, and the color is solid all the way through, making it less prone to bleaching. Asbestos shingle siding was also used heavily in the 1950s and 1960s and held up very well. Asbestos siding is fine as long as the siding is sealed with paint to prevent the asbestos fibers from flaking off. For information on asbestos, you can contact the Environmental Protection Agency at (202) 554-1404 for a booklet called "Asbestos in the Home" or the American Lung Association at (800) LUNG-USA for various other booklets about asbestos.

All sidings are fine as long as they are well maintained. Any wood siding can last for decades, but it must be treated every several years to keep the moisture out. All sidings must be sealed from penetrating moisture by caulking, sealing, and staining or painting. Check the flashing around the windows, door entrances, and corners. The flashing material is usually a metal such as aluminum that fits underneath the siding and is connected to the door frame or window frame. On the roof, the flashing will be used around a chimney or between two different levels of the roof. If the caulk or sealant is old or cracked, the siding is dry or water stained, or the paint is chipped, then the siding has not been well maintained.

While checking the siding, look up under the overhang (soffits) for the same problems. If the outside was not well maintained, chances are the inside of the house was not well maintained either. Pay particular attention to the areas just outside the kitchen and bathrooms. If there is no aluminum or paper **vapor barrier** outside these areas, excess moisture can allow condensation to collect inside the walls or on the back of the siding, leading to paint failure or rot.

Roof

Inspect the roof from the ground. Walk back away from the house far enough to see as much of it as you can. If the roofing material is laying flat and appears in good shape, it probably is. If it's a wood shingle roof, remember that wood must be treated and protected from moisture.

In some dry areas of the Southwest, wood roofs are not allowed owing to the potential fire hazard. If the roof is wood shingle and appears dry and cracked, have it inspected by a professional. Builders in the Southwest have switched to masonry tiles that come in a variety of colors and don't burn. Certain areas of California recently experienced major firestorms, and although the tile roofs fared better than the wood ones, blowing embers did infiltrate the gaps between the tiles, and the houses burned anyway. If the roof is not wood, masonry tile, or metal, then the roof is most likely either asphalt shingle or fiberglass.

If you see areas where the color has been bleached by the sun or where the corners of the roofing shingles have either bubbled or bent up, it may be time to replace the roof. Notice the areas around any chimneys or vents. Those areas are usually the worst for leaks. The flashing usually fits smoothly around metal chimneys and is caulked to seal against water. The flashing material will not fit as snugly against a masonry (stone or brick) chimney, and again that area must be sealed with caulking or liquid sealant. This type of sealant can dry out over time and cause leaks to develop around the flashing.

See if there are trees next to the house with limbs that extend over the roof. If you see mold on the roof, it is probably caused by those limbs blocking the sun and keeping the area from drying. Tree limbs also pose a potential lightning hazard, and, of course, the limb could fall onto the roof. The most annoying problem with tree limbs is that the leaves always fill the gutters in the fall, meaning that you must go up a ladder to clean them out. If you do not clean the gutters, water can fill them and freeze in the winter. Ice can then get under the roof shingles, and in the spring you may have an indoor shower where you did not plan one.

Exterior Windows and Doors

Before you enter the house, finish your inspection by checking the windows and doors. If the home is older, the windows may be **single glazed,** with a single pane of glass in each section. Check to see if the home comes with storm windows for each window. If the house is newer, you may find **double-glazed** windows, where two panes of glass are evident. Double glazed (often called **thermo-pane**) windows often take the form of a full glass window with the window grills built on the inside of the two panes; sometimes the grills are attached separately to the inside of the window. One of the most efficient insulators is **dead-air space.** Almost all types of insulators use this principle. In thermo-pane windows, the manufacturer creates a dead-air space between the two panes of glass by installing a rubber gasket around the panes and marrying them together, thereby sealing the windows from air infiltration around the panes. As you did with the siding, see if the windows are cracked or bent. When you are inside, check the windows to see if they close properly with a snug fit to the window sill.

Check the doors in the same way and make sure they close with a snug fit all around the doorjamb and along the door sill on the floor. Both windows and doors should fit tightly against a gasket of felt or vinyl to restrict air flow.

The two worst areas for air infiltration and heat loss are windows and doors. Most air leakage problems can be solved by, or reduced by, using a silicone sealant or weather stripping.

Interior Inspection

Most resale homes will be clean and sometimes freshly painted; occasionally, new carpet or vinyl flooring will have been installed. Remember Figure 4-1, which offers a parody of various people's perceptions. The same holds true when you are inspecting the interior of a house. If the house is still furnished, you may find the color coordination pleasing, or you may be impressed by how the location and quality of the furnishings creates a comfortable feeling in a room.

Your perception of that room or rooms can affect your perception of the entire house and inhibit any objections you may find. However, the furnishings you see will not be there when you move in with your own furnishings and the colors you see will probably change. Try to visualize the interior of the house without any furnishings at all. Paint and wallpaper can change, but the room sizes and locations will not unless you change them. What will the room look like with your colors and furniture?

You should inquire about the type of paint used on the interior walls and trim. Homes built before 1978 may have been painted with lead-based paint (LBP). Although most manufacturers stopped using lead in their paint in the 1950s, the federal government didn't ban it until 1978. For more information on the dangers of lead, contact the National Lead Information Center hotline at (800) 532-3394 or the Centers for Disease Control at (404) 488-7330.

Kitchens and Baths Sell Houses

You may hear the expression, "Kitchens and bathrooms sell houses." These areas will usually have the most custom items to show. The kitchen may have attractive cabinetry with a built-in niche for a microwave oven, a lazy Susan, or an attractive counter top.

The bathroom(s) may have attractive ceramic tile (check the grout for cracking or mold) or mirrored walls. You may also see an attractive fixture or a particular style of sink or tub in the bath that piques your interest.

Check the tub area. Are there sliding doors on the tub or shower, or is there just a shower curtain? If there are sliding doors, check the tracks where the door slides back and forth for dirt or wear. Check the areas where the tub and shower door frame meet for evidence of leaks.

Run the water in the sink and flush the toilet at the same time to see if the water pressure drops substantially when both are used. If there is a substantial drop in pressure, you do not want to be in the shower when someone starts the clothes washer.

With the possible exception of a living room or family room with a fireplace, kitchens and baths are where you will find more than just floors and walls, and thus they usually get much attention. But let's look for other things.

Look Up

Stand at the far end of a room and look at the ceiling. If there have been water problems or settling problems in the past, you may see where the ceiling has begun to sag. If the home was built with cathedral, tray, or vaulted ceilings, keep in mind that heat rises. High ceilings are definitely attractive, but if there is no provision for a ceiling fan or other device that will circulate the warm air that becomes trapped in those areas, pockets of warm, moist air will accumulate in the highest area of the ceiling and can rot the ceiling joists if not allowed to ventilate. With the rise of the warmer air, cooler air flows in to replace it, which can create a drafty floor area and therefore high heating bills. From an energy standpoint, high ceilings work better in areas such as the desert Southwest where you want the heat to rise above the living areas so that it can be circulated and cooled. They are attractive, but they are not free.

As you go through the house, you should check out the carpet and room colors, closet space, bathroom locations, room sizes (you should have a better feeling for room sizes if you have practiced at home), window locations, and the like. Pay more than a little attention to the size and location of the windows, not only for ventilation but for fire safety as well. At least one bedroom window should have at least an 18-inch free opening, which means that the window—when fully opened—should leave an open-space at least 18-inches in all four directions.

Climb Up

Check for ample closet space; we never seem to have enough. Check for an attic entry. Certain homes will have an attic stairway of either the built-in or pull-down variety. Other homes may have an opening in the ceiling called a **scuttle,** for which you will need a ladder to gain entry. Go into the attic and check the amount of insulation; an R-30 insulation factor requires at least nine inches of fiberglass-batt insulation. (**R-values** are heat- or cold-resistance values assigned to insulating materials—the higher the R-value, the better the insulation. If the home does not have at least nine inches of fiberglass, consider adding insulation if you buy that house. Check under the roof to see if the wood is discolored, which indicates a moisture problem or water leaking. If the wood is discolored, press your thumbnail or a screwdriver into the wood. Wood that flakes off or feels soft and spongy is probably rotten from moisture, or perhaps the house has an insect problem. Inspect the ceiling joists (if the attic does not have a finished floor) for the same type of damage.

You may not be able to conduct such a thorough inspection for each house you visit, but as you move through all the homes on your list, you will be able to keep an eye out for potential problems. When you choose the home you want, you can go back and do your complete inspection then.

Now we have inspected the outside, the living areas, and the attic. There's only one place left to go—to the basement.

Heating Systems

You need to pay attention to the various systems that allow the house to operate as a livable structure. Check the boiler or furnace to ensure that the heating system is in good shape; if the house has an electric heat system and is more than ten years old, have the system checked by an electrician to verify that the wiring is still safe. If the heating system is oil fired, find out how old it is, how often it was cleaned and maintained, and by whom. Oil-fired systems, unless they are fairly new, have a tendency to burn dirty unless they are tuned by a professional and maintained on a regular basis. Just as with your car, if you do not change the oil filters regularly, the engine will become dirty and eventually break down.

Gas heating systems tend to burn more cleanly and require less attention but need to be occasionally maintained and cleaned. You can generally tell how the system has been maintained by the amount of dust or soot in evidence near the furnace or by how the rest of the house was maintained. Ask how old the heating system is and what type of boiler or furnace it uses. Most heating systems installed since the 1960s have been hot-air or hot-water systems fueled by either oil or gas. Some hot-water systems have a heating coil built into the unit, and so you won't always see a water heater. Certain heating units have steel jackets inside them to mold the fire chamber. Although they work well, the steel units have a tendency to pit over time from the constant heating and cooling. The other type of jacket is made of cast iron; these are usually found in gas-fired units. Cast iron will suffer from pitting as well but usually lasts longer than the steel-cased units.

If the house has a hot-air system, check to see if there is a humidifier installed onto it. Hot-air systems have a tendency to make the air dry and allow the dust in the house to be constantly stirred up. They also have a tendency to make houses drafty because the warmest air flows from the vents closest to the furnace, leaving the cooler air to flow to the areas of the house furthest from it. To combat this problem, the heating ducts should be insulated to prevent heat loss as the air passes through them.

To keep the air from getting too dry, an automatic humidifier can be installed on the unit so that you can dial the amount of humidity you need. To combat the dust, you can install an electronic air cleaner that zaps the dust particles with positive or negative electricity, which causes them to adhere to a filter that can be washed off in your dishwasher. To combat the drafts, you can install a wedge, which is simply something four sided, flat, and about the same size as the duct work, into the heating duct to redirect the airflow from the warmest areas of the house to the areas that need more heat. It takes a while, but you will be able to provide the entire house with balanced, comfortable heat in a short time. "What a pain," you might say, "having to do all of that work!" Yes, but in the event you wish to install central air-conditioning, you will save several thousands of dollars in labor costs because the duct work will already be in place.

One danger from oil- or gas-fired heating systems is carbon monoxide. Using these fuels for heat and hot water requires the area where these units are placed to be *well ventilated with a fresh-air intake duct* to allow the heating systems to have enough air to function properly. If the heating units are starved for air, they will not burn cleanly and efficiently and may develop carbon deposits that will continue to make the unit burn less efficiently and thus produce carbon monoxide. For more information, you can contact the Consumer Product Safety Commission (CPSC) by writing to CPSC Publications Request, Washington, D.C. 20207. Another good source of information is your local fire inspector or building inspector, who is trained to inspect heating areas for construction code requirements.

Plumbing

Inspect the plumbing in the basement, under the sinks, in back of the toilets, and in the showers. If there has been a leak in the past, you should be able to see evidence of water damage or of repairs. If you see any such signs, ask the owner what caused them and when it was repaired. If the house is older, the waste lines could be made of cast iron. Inspect the pipes for rust, especially around the joints. If the water lines are made of galvanized steel, again, check for rust stains because you will be drinking from these pipes. A good place to find evidence of rust stains is the toilets and sinks, under the rims. Do not confuse rust stains with hard-water stains; I will cover hard water later.

Copper and polyvinylchloride (PVC), which is a fancy name for a type of plastic, are very resistant to rust and corrosion. In newer (post-1960s) homes, you are most likely to find copper water lines and PVC waste lines. PVC is also very inexpensive to buy and install.

Check the various faucets in the house to see if any of them leak. They may need a simple tightening, or you may need to replace a gasket. It is a good idea to insulate the hot-water lines with the foam-sleeve type of insulation available in most hardware stores. You want to make the home as energy efficient as you can not only to save money and the environment but also to increase resale value later on.

Check to see if there are any exterior water spigots. In areas prone to freezing temperatures, verify that all exterior spigots are either frost free or have an interior shut-off valve to prevent freezing. Ask the present owner or agent to locate all the interior shut-off valves for all water, oil, or gas lines. If there are only a few such valves, you might consider installing more so as to be able to control these lines if there is an emergency.

Run the water from several faucets simultaneously to determine if there is sufficient water pressure to run the dishwasher and take a shower at the same time. If the pipes are wrapped with asbestos insulation, as many were in homes built before the 1960s, you can contact the Environmental Protection Agency at (202) 554-1404 or the American Lung Association at (800) LUNG-USA for help on how to deal with this problem. If the pipes were soldered with lead, contact the National Lead Information Center Hotline at (800) 532-3394, the Centers for Disease Control at (404) 488-7330, the EPA Safe Drinking Water Hotline at (800) 426-4791, or you can obtain a test kit from Lead Test Kit at (704) 251-0518.

Water Heaters

If the home comes equipped with a water heater, find out whether it is electric, oil, or gas heated. If it is electric and the area is known for hard water, find out if it has been cleaned on a regular basis. Minerals in the water can react and adhere to the heating coils, thus shortening their life.

The same holds true for gas- and oil-fired heaters, although in those units the minerals settle to the bottom of the tank and build up. Inspect the tank for rust or corrosion, especially on the bottom or around the drains. If rust or corrosion is evident, you may have to replace the unit. Gas- or oil-fired units should be maintained in the same way as a furnace or boiler. Normally, a 30-gallon capacity is sufficient for the average family. If there is no separate water-heating unit, the water may be heated by a quick-recovery coil built into the boiler. These coils work well, but you may run out of hot water if the dishwasher is running at the same time you take your shower.

Just like their air-heating cousins, gas- and oil-fired water heaters pose a risk of emitting carbon monoxide if not properly vented and maintained.

Basement Walls and Floors

While you're in the basement, inspect the foundation walls to see if there are any cracks or settling spots. If you saw a crack outside and you see another crack inside in the same area, then the crack could go all the way through the wall, which would be a big problem. Also check the floor joists (beams) over your head. In older homes there may not be any insulation, and the beams and the floorings are exposed. If the floors upstairs are covered, you can see the type of subfloor used when the house was built. In an older home you may see individual boards, usually oak, that were originally laid down as a hardwood floor and eventually covered up. In newer homes, you should see the bottom of the plywood floor used as a subfloor. Plywood is fine and has been used in thousands of homes without a problem. However, because of federal and state energy codes that require insulation of at least R-11 or 3.5 inches of fiberglass or equivalent installed on the basement ceiling, you may have to search for the subfloor in newer homes. Or the lower level could have been finished off as living space, and so the subfloor is covered up. If in doubt, ask the owner. If you can see the first floor joists, inspect them as you did the roof rafters for damage caused by moisture or insects.

If you can, take a look along the top of the foundation where the concrete meets the wood. Check for evidence of mouse droppings or dead insects like carpenter ants or termites. You can also find dead insects in spider webs around any area that produces dampness like the water heater or well-pump storage tank. If you see evidence of carpenter ants, termites, or powderpost beetles, ask the owner about the problem and what has been done about it, if anything. Figure 6-6 illustrates how to identify which pest is in residence by the sort of damage each causes.

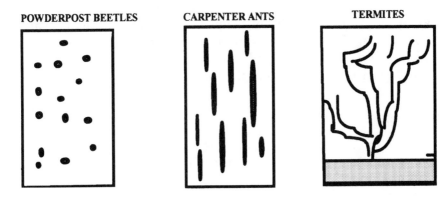

Figure 6-6.   Damage to wood from powderpost beetles, carpenter ants, and termites.

Carpenter ants burrow into the wood, forming channels, especially in damp areas around windows and doors and in basements, and leaving piles of chewed wood that resemble small piles of sawdust. Carpenter ants are usually black in color and much larger than their cousins.

Termites burrow into and eat the wood along its grain, creating dark bulges or blisters filled with tunnels that resemble small galleries. Termites leave behind discarded wings and fecal pellets that resemble small seeds. Ground termites build mudlike tubes from the underground nest up the foundation wall and into the wood.

Powderpost beetles bore into the wood and lay their eggs. The larvae feed on the wood as they grow and exit the wood as adults, leaving small round holes and piles of chewed wood resembling powder.

Check the edge of the basement concrete slab where the floor meets the wall. If you see any areas of water stains, have it checked out. A water stain might show up as a discoloration in the concrete, or you might notice an area that looks like white mold. That white substance may be the lime leaching out of the concrete, which usually occurs in damp areas.

Sometimes during unusual periods of extensive rain, the drains fill up, and water finds its way into the foundation. This happened to me recently. An unusually heavy snow accumulation was quickly melted by warm spring rains. The soil (mostly clay) could not absorb that much water, the drains all filled beyond capacity, and the water found its way into the basement. Actually, the weight of the house pressing down on the soil forced the water through the seams between the basement walls and the floor. To relieve the situation, we had to dig a new trench and install a new drain at a lower elevation, which allowed the water to drain away. I'm glad the lot was not flat.

Electricity

You must verify that the house has enough electrical power to meet your needs. Let's review some of the terminology that you'll need to know:

- **Ampere (amp):** The amount of current flowing past a given point at a given time. Each electrical device has a certain amperage rating, and each circuit is rated for the total number of amperes it can safely deliver. Household amperage ratings are usually between 50 and 200 amps.

- **Circuit:** A continuous path for an electrical current.
- **Current:** The movement of electrons (electricity) measured in amperes.
- **Volt:** A measurement of the strength or pressure of an electrical current. Household circuits are usually 120 or 240 volts.
- **Watt:** The rate at which electrical devices consume energy; the power produced by a one-ampere current across a potential difference of one volt.

Electrical current flows on a continuous path from the power company, through the electric meter, and into the main service panel in your home. The main service panel may contain fuses (for most homes built before 1960) or circuit breakers. At the panel, the power is separated into branch circuits and distributed throughout the house.

The branch circuits may be wired with either aluminum or copper wire or a combination of both. You should try to establish how the circuits are divided throughout the house. Each circuit, depending on its intended use, will carry a particular size of wire and will be wired into the panel box into a certain amp-rated fuse or circuit breaker.

If you overload the circuit by plugging in too many appliances or if an appliance has a short in it, the surge of excess power will cause a metal strip in the fuse to overheat and melt, and the circuit will be broken. The circuit breaker will "trip," or shut down, the circuit in the same way.

You should have the wiring inspected and the circuits tested to make sure they are active, especially if the house is several decades old. The National Electrical Code now requires that ground-fault circuit interruptors (GFCIs) be installed in all panel boxes.

The GFCI is a highly sensitive breaker that measures the current entering and leaving a device along a circuit. If the difference is greater than 0.007 amperes, the breaker will trip and interrupt the circuit. GFCI wall outlets are now also mandatory within six feet of the kitchen-sink and in bathrooms, garages, basements, and exterior outlets. Most homes built before 1983 were serviced by at least 50 to 100 amps. Because of the growing number of home electronic devices that require more circuits and thus larger panel boxes, most builders have switched to at least 200-amp service.

You should check to make sure that the service provided in the home will meet your needs. Also check to see how many circuits are provided in high-use areas, such as the kitchen, bathrooms, and garage. If you have a single circuit in the kitchen that services the refrigerator, dishwasher, and toaster at the same time, you may find the circuit overloaded if you plug in one more appliance. Make sure that all power is off when you are changing fuses or breakers by shutting off the main switch to the box. Review this procedure with the building inspector or fire inspector before you try it on your own.

Make sure the house is properly grounded. You should see a wire protruding from under the siding that is attached to a copper rod that extends into the ground. If you cannot find the grounding rod, ask the owner how and where the house is grounded.

Windows

There are a variety of types of windows in use today. The best insulator is solid wood; however, solid wood may not be practical in areas of high moisture or humidity. Remember, there is no such thing as maintenance-free wood. If the wood is exposed to the elements, it will need to be maintained. Wood windows must be painted, caulked, and sealed against the weather. Aluminum windows are normally maintenance free, with the paint baked on, but they tend to accumulate condensation on the inside of the window jamb. The outside of the window is exposed to the cold, which is transmitted to the inside. Moisture in the inside air from cooking, washing, and showers condenses on the glass and runs down onto the window sill. If the sill is made of something other than ceramic or stone, the water may stain and rot the sill. To combat this problem, manufacturers of aluminum windows have installed insulation inside the window jambs called **thermo-breaks.**

Another type of window introduced several years ago is the vinyl-clad window. These windows are good insulators and reduce condensation on the jambs. Certain windows are manufactured with vinyl exteriors and wood interiors. This has been the most popular type since they were first introduced. You can paint or stain the interior to match your decor, and the outside of the window comes in several colors to match your exterior decor. Some of the most popular windows available today are vinyl-clad exterior, wood-interior, thermo-pane, high-performance windows. No, you cannot take these windows for a high-speed spin around the track.

The high-performance window has a microscopically thin metallic coating bonded to an inner surface of the sealed pane of glass that restricts the flow of heat through the dead-air space between the two panes of glass. Besides this feature, some manufacturers have filled the dead-air space with argon gas to restrict the transmission of heat from the inside of the home. Don't panic—argon is an inert gas, which means it has certain properties that restrict air flow through it. We breathe argon every day as part of the mixture of gases that make up our atmosphere.

In areas such as the Southwest, where summer temperatures can reach 120 degrees, this combination of applications can save you money in heating and cooling expenses. In addition, certain manufacturers offer tinted coatings, similar to the ones you see in late-model cars, to deflect the sun's rays and thereby lower the heat gain.

Windows are also classified according to how they open. In **single-hung windows,** the top sash is stationary or fixed and the bottom sash moves up or down; in **double-hung windows,** both the top and bottom sash move up or down. **Casement windows** will crank out from left to right or the reverse. **Awning windows** crank out from the bottom or top, and **sliding windows** slide from left to right or vice versa. I have found that the single- or double-hung window is the most popular in the Northeast, partly owing to its popularity among builders and partly owing to the increased cost of the other kinds of windows. There are other types of windows available in various sizes and shapes that can greatly enhance the appearance of the home; however, if your pocket book is not bulging with cash, you may be satisfied with the standard types.

All forms of insulation have an **R-value,** which is a measurement of their ability to resist heat and cold. The higher the R-value, the greater the insulation efficiency. The R-value in a window pertains to the resistance value in the center of the glass. The center of glass R-value for an Anderson©-Perma-Shield-Narrowline™ window is 4.2 according to a study of the window done by Lawrence Berkeley Labs, copyrights by Anderson Window Corporation, Bayport, MN, 1992.

Doors

Exterior doors are often made of solid wood, which, as was just mentioned, is an excellent insulator. There are also models that are steel clad with a foam core, and recently fiberglass doors have been manufactured to resemble wood (these are also foam cored). Insulated garage doors are also available. Most glass doors, such as the common sliding variety, have an R-value comparable to similar windows and are subject to the same limitations as aluminum- and wood-frame windows.

Although solid wood is a great insulator, totally sealing wood doors against the weather is almost impossible unless done by a manufacturer. It is also difficult to weather-strip a wooden door against air infiltration, because the wood will swell in areas of high humidity, shrink in areas of low humidity, and dry and crack in areas of high heat and low humidity.

I have tried metal, foam, and felt weather stripping, and I have found that felt and foam work the best. Steel doors with internal poly-foam insulation with factory-installed vinyl weather strippings are very good at stopping the flow of air if installed properly. The average R-value provided by these doors is 14.5.

Insulation

As I mentioned in the section on windows, dead air is a great insulator. Almost all forms of insulation are based on this premise. The most popular form of wall and ceiling insulation used today is the **fiberglass batt.** The fiberglass is formed in such a way as to produce extremely fine fibers, almost like human hair, and cut into sections to form batts, or layers, of various sizes.

When I built new homes in the late 1970s in my area of southern New York State, the federal insulation requirements were that walls had to have an R-value of 11 (R-11), equivalent to 3.5 inches of fiberglass; ceilings had to be R-19, equivalent to 6.25

inches of fiberglass; and floors (basement ceilings) had to be R-11. The most common construction material used for wall construction at that time was the 2″ × 4″ stud.

When the new federal energy codes were enacted in early 1976, partly due to the rise in oil prices and the nation's burgeoning awareness of the need to protect the environment, the required R-values changed. The minimum wall insulation factor increased to R-19, the floor requirement stayed at R-11, and the ceiling requirement increased to R-30, which is equivalent to nine inches of fiberglass. To achieve the increase in R-values without increasing the size of the lumber itself (and thereby substantially increasing the cost of the house), several manufacturers introduced **insulated sheathing.**

Sheathing is the material used to wrap the exterior walls of the house to cut down on air infiltration and moisture. Plywood wrapped with tar paper used to be the most common sheathing used. Insulated sheathing consisted of two pieces of aluminized foil with a poly-foam insulation product sandwiched in the middle and had an average R-value of 5, which brought the overall wall R-value to 16 (R-11 + R-5). To achieve the balance of the insulation needed, the builders' engineers calculated the R-values of the siding, foil backing, paper vapor barriers on the fiberglass, and Sheetrock on the inside of the house to reach the federally mandated total of 19. However, this formula was debatable.

Many builders, preferring to keep it simple and to enhance their chances of finding a buyer, started advertising houses constructed with 2″ × 6″ exterior walls with a full batt of 6.25-inch (R-19) fiberglass insulation. This type of construction became very popular with most buyers, because 2″ × 6″ walls sounded much more substantial than 2″ × 4″ walls, and its popularity continues today.

The exterior walls do not supply much more support than the siding because the actual structural lumber used in building the frame absorbs almost all the stress. The 2″ × 8″ floor joist with R-11 has remained, and the ceiling joists have increased to 2″ × 8″ to accommodate the 9.5 inches needed to achieve the required R-30. Structural lumber has also changed in recent years owing to its required increase in size. Floor joists, for example, have increased from 2″ × 8″ to 2″ × 10″ or even larger.

In turn-of-the-century homes, it is not uncommon to find that the only built-in insulation feature is an area to create dead air between the walls. Sometimes that space is filled with hay or even horse hair. To combat this lack of insulation, there are a variety of cellulose insulations that can be blown in from the outside to fill the space. The overall key to a well-insulated home is to stop the heat or cold from coming in and going out.

Don't Seal It Completely

To completely seal the house from any air infiltration at all is dangerous. The house must breathe just like you and me. I have seen new homes that have been wrapped with plastic sheets like a Christmas package to seal out the cold—and seal in moisture. The plastic not only sealed out the cold but also sealed in all the moisture created by washing, cooking, showering, and so on. The interior walls of the house began to grow mold because they never dried out.

You also must breathe while you're inside the house, especially during the heating season in colder climates. Household items produce all kinds of pollutants, such as carpet fibers, Sheetrock particles, carbon dioxide, and chemicals from cleaning fluids. Everything breaks down over time; we need a certain amount of fresh air inside the home to replace the stale air we create. Insulate all you want, but do not seal up the house entirely.

Ventilation

Look at the top of the roof. Since the 1970s, it's been a common practice to install a **continuous-ridge vent** in new homes. This type of vent is made of metal or plastic and runs along the very top of the roof to allow hot, moist air accumulated in the attic to escape. If this hot, moist air cannot escape, condensation can build up and rot the roof rafters and ceiling joists.

In some parts of the Southwest that are warm during the day yet cool off dramatically overnight, condensation can quickly build up in the warm attic space if the air cannot escape. I have seen homes in which moisture stains were visible on the ceiling; upon inspection of the attic, I found condensation forming on the tips of the roofing nails and dripping down like rain onto the insulation.

If your home does not have a continuous-ridge vent, you may see vents installed just under the peak of the roof on each end of the house. These are called **gable-end vents.** In more contemporary homes with many peaks and valleys in the roof lines, you may find a variety of venting systems. And if your home was built before the 1970s and has a cathedral or tray-type ceiling, make sure that the insulation in that high ceiling is not installed tightly against the underside of the roof sheathing. If air is not allowed to pass between the roof and the insulation, condensation will form and the wood will rot. In newer homes, a styrofoam tray known as an **eave baffle** is installed between the roof and insulation to allow the hot, moist air to flow to the roof vents.

Fiberglass insulation comes in batts of various sizes, with R-values from 11 to 38. I believe that one should have at least an R-19 exterior wall and an R-38 ceiling in any area of the country. The insulation not only keeps out the cold but also retains the air-conditioned cool air in areas of extreme summer heat. Fiberglass insulation combined with thermo-pane windows and insulated exterior doors should keep your home comfortable and energy efficient, with a payback to compensate for the added cost—a well-insulated house will earn you additional money upon resale because the purchaser will also enjoy the benefits.

In any home, new or old, you should always strive to obtain the things you need before the things you want. If you opt to install that new swimming pool instead of repairing the windows or installing better insulation, the costs of operating a low-efficiency home will make the overall cost of that pool much higher than necessary.

Decks and Patios

Inspect the deck carefully. If it was built with wood that was not **pressure treated** with chemicals to inhibit moisture damage, make sure the wood is still in good shape and has not begun to rot. If the deck sits on concrete pillars, make sure they are straight up and down and not tilted. If the deck sits on a concrete block, make sure the block is straight and stable. Inspect the plate where the deck is connected to the house. The deck should be **bolted** to the side of the house; if there are only nails, be very careful. The last thing you need is to have your housewarming party congregate on your deck and then fall into the back yard. This has happened more than once. Make sure the bolts and the plate are in good shape; if they are rusted or the plate is cracked, they should be replaced.

If the house has a concrete or stone patio, check the concrete for cracking. A certain amount of cracking is acceptable as long as the cracks are not more than 1/32 of an inch wide and allow water to filter down under the concrete, and even those should be sealed with a concrete sealer. If the concrete or stone has cracked and is uneven or not level, there is a good chance that water has infiltrated and either washed out sections of ground underneath or frozen, pushing up and cracking the concrete or mortar. Uneven sections are dangerous when guests are walking or children are playing. The problem will only get worse until it is repaired.

Fire Safety

All homes should be equipped with at least one smoke detector, which is usually mounted at the top of the stairs leading to the bedrooms in a two-story home. In a one-story home, the smoke detector should be mounted on the wall in the hall just outside the bedroom area. In newer homes, smoke detectors are a mandatory federal requirement. They are usually wired into the house, with a battery backup in case the power goes out.

If the home has no smoke detector at all, there are many types available at your local building material stores and hardware stores. They are easy to install and are battery operated. I recommend that you place at least one in the hall near the bedroom area and another one high up on the wall or on the ceiling just outside the furnace area.

Another area of concern is the garage, which is normally used for the storage of automobiles, lawn tractors, paint cans, and a myriad of other flammable products. In older homes, you might find a simple wooden door between the house and garage. You should have a fire door installed or have the old door brought up to fire code by installing a metal sheet over the garage side of the door. The door should have a burn rating of at least 90 minutes, which means that if a fire starts in the garage, the door should be able to withstand the heat for at least 90 minutes before allowing the fire to burn through.

If your garage is attached to the house, the wall that is attached to the house should be covered with fire-code Sheetrock. Its actual burn rating will depend not only on the Sheetrock but also on what system of framing and insulation is behind it. It is best to ask your local fire inspector to recommend a wall system for you to use. Usually, fire-code Sheetrock that is at least 5/8 inch thick applied to both sides of the wall that is attached to the garage can give you a 60-minute burn rate. If you cannot cover the inside wall, you can double up on the wall in the garage. For homes with a built-in garage, also known as **garage under** homes, the entire inside of the garage should be covered with fire-coded Sheetrock. If the walls are constructed of concrete and the ceiling is wood frame, just the ceiling need be covered and sealed against fire.

The furnace, boiler, and water heater area should also be covered with fire-code Sheetrock. If the heating system is in the basement, the same requirements apply as in the garage. If the heating system is installed within the living areas of the home, the entire area should be protected against fire. Remember that all of the fire-coded materials are fire retardant, *not* fire proof. They may slow the fire down, but they will not stop it.

Locate the best escape routes from the house if there is a fire. Make sure that the windows operate freely without sticking and that no doorways to the outside are blocked or hard to open. One window in each room should have at least an 18-inch free opening, which means that the window sash, when opened fully, should measure at least 18 inches in all directions to allow enough room for an average-sized person to crawl through.

I also strongly recommend you **get a professional opinion.** Call your local fire inspector and ask him to come over, go through the house, and make recommendations. Ask the inspector for **child-location stickers** to be placed on the windows of the children's rooms. Ask for instructions on what to do if there is a fire and make sure that all members of your family are present for the instructions.

Water and Sewer Systems

If your home is located within a municipal water and sewer district, you don't have to worry about the amount of water available unless there is a drought or the area in general has a low level of available water. In certain areas of the Southwest, there is no water at all, not even in the ground; water must be trucked in and stored in tanks on the property.

Despite dry periods or occasional drops in pressure, municipal systems usually accommodate the needs of their citizens. The same holds true for municipal sewer systems unless the area has experienced enough growth to force the expansion or construction of sewer treatment plants. The advantage of municipal systems is that most of the worry is experienced by the municipality; the disadvantage is that you have to pay for this convenience by paying a fee. The same is true if your house is part of a privately held central water and sewer system, as may be the case in areas where municipal systems are not available. And although municipal systems are very convenient, the quality of the water may not be to your liking, because it must be treated to remove various bacteria and minerals (see chapter 9).

All water comes from Mother Nature. Large cities and towns draw their water from large lakes and rivers called **reservoirs,** which are usually located outside of town, or from **watersheds** in mountainous regions, where snow melt combines with rainfall to produce enough water to meet local residents' needs. The water is drawn from the reservoirs or watersheds through aqueducts or large pipes down to the municipalities' treatment plants and from there to homes and businesses.

Another source of water for municipalities is underground water, which can be accessed by drilling wells. If the municipality tests to find an underground river or aquifer and discovers that there is enough to serve the community, the water is drawn up and pumped to the treatment plant.

One incident that prompted me to write this book was the response I received to an ad I recently placed to sell a building lot. The customer called me on the phone and asked about the availability of water and sewer services. I informed him that the area did not have a municipal system and that the lot would have to be served by an individual well and septic tank. He had been born and raised in New York City, where all he had to do to obtain water was turn on the faucet, so he asked me, "With a well, where does the water come from?" That question may sound silly to some, but I have found that many of my customers are apprehensive when municipal water and sewer systems are not available because they simply do not understand how a private well and septic system works. If you are one of those people, all will be explained to you in chapter 9.

Now that you have thoroughly inspected the property, you need to calculate its worth.

HOW DO I QUALIFY THE HOUSE'S PRICE?

You will undoubtedly visit more than just a few homes. Like the appraiser, you will have to make note of the various amenities each home offers, judge its general condition and asking price, and discuss the sale prices for other, similar homes in the general area.

What a home is worth to you basically depends on whether the home meets your needs and has something of what you want, as well as on how much you can afford to pay and what you are willing to pay.

It would be great if you underpaid for a house and not so great if you overpaid. My experience has taught me that there is always some room for negotiation in every deal. The key is to establish the actual value of the property as accurately as possible. You shouldn't mind paying for what the property is worth, and if you can estimate the value, you minimize the risk of paying too much.

If you have qualified the area, the neighborhood, the site, and the house, it should not be difficult to establish the range of value. Here's a valuable tip: If you have found that perfect house, wait at least a day before you make your offer unless homes in the area are selling like hot cakes and you simply can't chance losing it. Go over your list of pros and cons and review the house again in your mind. If you need to, ask the agent to arrange another inspection to refresh your opinion and be comfortable with your choice. With that information in mind, you can begin your negotiations, which you'll learn about in chapter 14.

Is the Paperwork in Order?

In most areas of the country, municipalities have enacted zoning laws governing everything from the size of the building lots and the actual use of the land to the size and color of for-sale signs. Zoning is covered in chapter 11.

Included in most zoning ordinances are requirements to obtain permits to perform certain work or improvements to property within the various zones. The ordinance may require that to change or add something to the property, a detailed plan must be submitted to the town, certain fees must be paid, permits must be issued, inspections must be performed by the municipal building inspector, and documents of completion (also known as certificates of occupancy, or c-of-os) must be signed and approved by the inspector's office.

If the home you are interested in has added features, such as a garage, swimming pool, patio, deck, or storage building, ask the owner whether these features were originally built with the house or were added later. If they were added after the original house was completed, it is possible that to construct them would have required the municipality's approval according to the local zoning law.

Ask for copies of the application, permits, and certificate of occupancy or completion. If the owner cannot produce the documents, contact the local building inspector's office and ask to obtain copies. All of this information is public information. If you have illegal additions on the property, you cannot obtain a **clear title,** and without a clear title, you cannot close the mortgage. Titles are covered in chapter 12.

Ask the owner or agent if there are warranties for any appliances, water heaters, heating or cooling systems, new siding or roofing, or anything else that can be transferred to you. Sometimes the owner has paid for extended warranties for certain items, and he may allow those warranties to transfer to you for free or for a price.

Ask to see a copy of the survey for the property. The **survey** shows the lot's boundaries as well as the exact locations of the house, the driveway, the well or water and sewer lines, and sometimes the location and size of the septic fields. Surveys are described in chapter 10.

Check the date on the survey and see if there have been any additions or alterations to the lot or house since it was done. This will give you a good indication as to whether there are potential zoning or building violations. If there are violations, contact the building inspector and find out what can be done to correct the situation. The seller is responsible for selling you the house in a marketable condition.

Lot Lines

Ask the owner or agent to show you the **boundary lines** (also known as **lot lines**) of the property on the survey and then ask him to show you the actual boundaries by walking the boundaries of the property with you. You may find that the current or former owner has cleared beyond his property line to allow his kids more room to play or for some other, similar reason. This is not unusual because most surveyors use wooden lathes called **survey stakes** to mark a lot's boundaries, and subsequently the lathe is either taken out of the ground or rots away. Most surveyors also drive metal pins near the stakes, but these are very hard to find without a metal detector.

Check Figure 6-7 to see how the owners of property adjoining vacant lots have a tendency to clear a little bit more every year, thus making their yard appear larger every year. This is a common occurrence and can be rectified with a certified survey.

By walking the property line, you can see where the property begins and ends and sometimes, if you can find the pins, you will find that the lot is not as big or small as you first thought.

If there is no current survey available, try the local assessor's office and ask for a copy of the current tax map, which will show the location of the house and the property lines with fairly accurate dimensions.

One full acre measures 43,560 square feet. Using the KISS theory, builders came up with a "builders acre" or "short acre" to make it easier to judge the approximate size of a property. A short acre is 40,000 square feet; a perfect short acre measures 200 feet wide by 200 feet long or deep.

When you are looking at properties, you don't need to know the exact square footage of each lot to get an idea of its approxi-

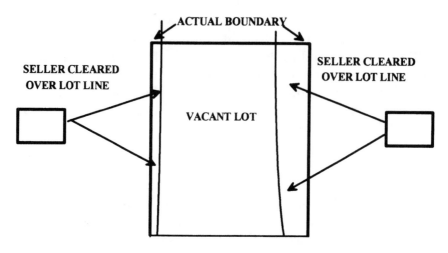

Figure 6-7. Overclearing.

mate size. Use the short acre as a guide. If one acre is about 40,000 square feet, than a half acre is about 20,000 square feet, a quarter acre is about 10,000 square feet, and a third of an acre is about 13,000 square feet. If you find a property you like, refer to the survey to calculate the exact square footage of the lot. By using the short acre method, you will have enough information to qualify the property without becoming buried beneath a pile of descriptive documents.

Inspection Checklist

Review Figure 6-8 and use it as you visit each house. Check off the listed items and indicate their condition using a colored pen or highlighter. If, at the end of the visit, you have more check-marks in the "poor" column, reconsider buying that house. If you have more checkmarks in the "acceptable" column, it's time for compromise with future repairs in mind. If the condition is good or excellent overall, attach a photo of the house to this checklist and review all the houses you have visited when you get back home.

Figure 6-8. Home inspection checklist.

Address _____

Price _____ Age _____

Broker _____ Phone _____

Date visited _____ Liked—yes/no? _____

Lot Size—⅓ acre ☐ ½ acre ☐ ¾ acre ☐ 1 acre ☐ Other _____

House style _____ Overall square footage _____

Number of bedrooms ___ Number of Baths ___ Tubs ___ Showers ___

Circle correct choice   *Check appropriate box*

	Excel-lent	*Good*	*Accept-able*	*Poor*
Lot elevation for drainage				
Driveway (gravel/black-top/clay)				
Foundation (block/poured/slab-up)				
Siding (wood/mason/vinyl/other)				
Roof (wood/asphalt/fiberglass/masonry)				
Roof (ridge vent/gable-end vent)				
Windows (single-hung/double-hung/case/slide)				
Windows (wood/aluminum/vinyl)				
Doors (wood/steel/sliding glass)				
Interior walls (Sheetrock/plaster/paint/wallpaper)				
Interior floors (hardwood/carpet/tile/ceramic/vinyl)				
Living room				

Figure 6-8. *(Continued)*

	Excel- lent	Good	Accept- able	Poor
Dining room				
Family room				
Kitchen				
Baths				
Bedrooms				
Kitchen and bath cabinets				
Kitchen faucet: (Single/ double)				
Kitchen range: (wall oven/ dishwasher/trash com- pactor)				
Kitchen refrigerator (16 cu.ft./18 cu.ft./20 cu.ft.)				
Kitchen sink (single/ double/steel/porcelain)				
Kitchen counter (formica/ ceramic/other)				
Powder room (ceramic/ mason/tile)				
Guest bathroom (ceramic/ mason/tile/wood)				
Guest bathroom (tub/ shower/fiberglass/steel)				
Master bathroom (ceramic/ tile/mason/other)				
Master bathroom (shower/ tub/steel/fiberglass)				
Master bathroom (Jacuzzi/ hot tub/other)				

Figure 6-8. *(continued)*

	Excel-lent	Good	Accept-able	Poor
Master bathroom (single-double sinks/porcelain/marble)				
Heating (oil/gas/electric/pump)				
Heating (hot water/hot air)				
Hot water (tank/built-in coil)				
Air-conditioning (central/thru wall/swamp system)				
Fireplace(s)				
Other custom features				

7

RADON

Although radon was discovered in 1900 by a German physicist who first thought it to be no more than a rare form of gas, we know today that it can pose a serious health threat if allowed to accumulate in our homes.

Upon leaving work one day in 1984, an engineer at a nuclear power plant in Pennsylvania with an accident-free work record set off the alarm on a newly installed radiation monitor. The engineer was decontaminated and sent home; however, the alarms sounded the next day and the next and the next—every time the engineer passed through the monitor. Occasionally, the monitor showed that the engineer was carrying six times more radiation than was considered safe. No one could figure out how he was being regularly exposed to radiation.

One day, late in the year, the engineer decided to enter the building a different way and passed through the exit door, where a new radiation monitor was installed, instead of the entrance. The monitor alarms went off again, but he was entering the building, not exiting. What could this mean?

It was finally concluded that the only place this employee could have picked up any radiation was somewhere in or near his home. Investigators were sent in, and they discovered that the radiation level in the living room of his house measured 700 times higher than the maximum level considered safe for human beings. The radiation was produced by radon gas.

It is helpful to understand how this radiation is produced even though, because we're not rocket scientists, the names of these elements sound like ancient Greek gods.

Radon is one of the many natural by-products of the isotope radium-226, which changes into other elements while giving off bits of pure energy called radiation as it decays. These by-products are technically known as radon progenies and include the radioactive elements polonium-218, lead-214, bismuth-214, and polonium-214. These elements have very short half-lives and can continue to exist only in radon, which itself has a half-life of 3.82 days (the half-life is the amount of time it takes for one-half of the atoms in a radioactive substance to disintegrate). The progenies are ultrafine heavy metals that can become electrically charged and attach themselves to dust particles, clothes, furniture, and air passages in the lungs where they continue to give off radiation. The particular isotope that we are concerned about is known as radon-222.

Without getting too complicated, the major worry for a homeowner is that radon gas, which is colorless and odorless, can accumulate in the home and cause physical harm. To obtain more information on radon, you can contact the American Lung Association at (800) LUNG-USA or the EPA's radon hotline at (800) SOS-RADON, which is the same number for the National Safety Council. There is also a new publication available from the EPA called "The Home Buyer's and Seller's Guide to Radon" that provides information about indoor testing.

HOW DO I FIND IT?

Approximately 100,000 homes have been tested thus far out of more than 70 million homes in the United States. It has been concluded that radon can be found almost anywhere that radium-bearing rock is located. Deposits of granite, shale, and phosphate are all potential sources of radon; however, the gas remains elusive. Although the Pennsylvania engineer's home was found to have radon levels more than 2,000 times higher than normal, another home located less than 100 feet away was tested and found to be free of radon.

The only way to be sure is to conduct a test on your own or have someone test for you. The basement or crawlspace area is the best place to test, because the gas seeps up from the ground through the cracks and seams in the foundation or floor. As warm air within the house rises, it creates a vacuum effect that draws the radon into the lowest levels of the house. Slab-on-grade or slab-up houses have more protection from the gas because the lowest level of these houses is usually on or above ground level. However, radon can still seep up through the concrete slab if cracks in it are not sealed.

With the advent of the new energy codes of 1976 and the increases in the price of heating fuel and gasoline, we all became more energy conscious. Builders began to incorporate energy-saving features into new homes, such as heavier insulation, thicker walls, and energy-efficient windows and doors. This was great for saving money and the environment, but these improvements allow radon to accumulate that much faster, because the houses do not "breathe" as much as they used to.

TESTING DEVICES

There are two types of devices used to test for radon. The **passive radon-testing devices** do not need power to function; examples include **charcoal canisters, alpha-track detectors,** and **charcoal-liquid scintillation devices** that are available in most hardware stores or by mail. Another passive device, the **electric ion chamber,** is usually available only through laboratories. These devices are placed in the lowest level of the house that is suitable for occupancy and are exposed to the air for a specified period of time.

The Environmental Protection Agency (EPA) recommends a multistage testing process. Stage one is the screening test to determine if high concentrations of radon exist in the home. If the reading for stage one equals 0.02 working level (WL), which equals 4 picocuries per liter of air (pCi/l) or below, the EPA recommends that follow-up tests should be performed at your discretion. If the results are between 0.02 and 0.01 WL (4 to 20 pCi/l), the EPA says that you should be concerned about long-term exposure to radon.

There are also **active devices** that can be used, such as **continuous radon monitors** and **continuous working monitors** that require a power supply and a trained technician. These devices offer the most extensive interference-dampening features to ensure that environmental factors such as excessive heat or humidity do not alter the results. Although they may cost more, they will offer more reliable information.

Remember to take into account the time of year when you are testing. In colder climates, radon levels may be higher during the winter months because houses are closed up and not often ventilated.

The EPA suggests two short-term testing options, because time is usually short when you are buying a home and no one has time to wait for lengthy tests. Use a passive device to take the initial test for at least 48 hours. After the first test, take a follow-up test (or two) for another 48 hours. If the average level of radon is 4 pCi/l or more, the radon level will have to be lowered.

The other test has to be with an active testing device with a continuous monitor for at least 48 hours.

HOW DO I FIX IT?

The easiest way to remove radon from the home is to ventilate naturally by opening the windows. Unfortunately, this remedy is not very practical and can triple your heating or cooling expenses. The average home will undergo at least one air change per hour (ACH), and certain older homes may even undergo two ACHs. However, since the energy-saving craze in the 1970s, newer tightly-built or reinsulated homes have reduced their airloss to 0.5 ACH, thereby increasing their efficiency and trapping more radon.

Because radon seeps in through cracks and seams, the first step in eliminating it is to seal those areas. This will help to stop the infiltration, but it is **not** recommended as the sole solution by the EPA.

You should hire a qualified contractor who has been state certified to do the job. The EPA requires contractors to take training courses through its Radon Contractor Proficiency Program (RCP) and pass an exam before they can be listed in the EPA's National RCP Report. RCP contractors carry a photo identification card and are required to follow EPA regulations to make sure their work meets requisite quality standards. Certain states have their own contractor certification programs that may have additional requirements.

The cost to reduce the radon in a home can run as low as $500 or as high as $2,500, depending on the characteristics of the house and choice of methods. Most radon-reduction systems will cause an increase in your heating or cooling costs.

The type of system you should use depends on whether the house was built on a slab, with a crawlspace, or with a full foundation. A contractor can perform a visual inspection of the house and design a system tailored to its specific features. If the physical inspection fails to provide enough information, the contractor may need to perform a diagnostic test to help determine the best system for the job.

One such diagnostic test involves using a smoke gun to determine the air flow by watching small amounts of smoke that have been shot into holes, drains, and sump pumps or along cracks and seams. Another is the **soil communication test,** in which a vacuum cleaner hose is inserted into a small hole and a smoke gun blows smoke into a second small hole. The contractor can determine the drift of the air by observing if the smoke is drawn by the suction made by the vacuum cleaner.

RADON-REDUCTION TECHNIQUES

For full-foundation or slab-up homes, there are four types of soil suction used. **Active subslab suction** (also called **subslab depressurization**) is the most common and reliable reduction method. Suction pipes are inserted through the floor slab into the crushed rock or soil underneath. The pipes also may be inserted below the concrete slab from the outside of the house. A fan is connected to the pipes that acts like a vacuum cleaner and draws the gas from below the house into the open air as shown in Figure 7-1. **Passive subslab suction** works the same way, except that it relies on natural air currents instead of a fan.

Drain tile suction is another way to reduce radon. It works on the same principle as subslab suction except that the fan is con-

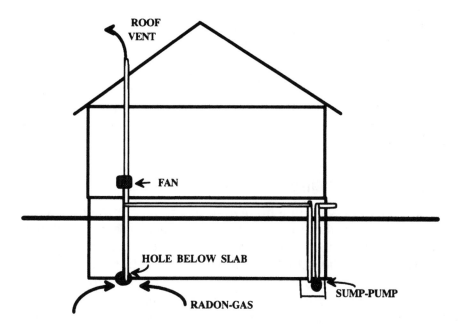

ROOF VENT

FAN

HOLE BELOW SLAB

RADON-GAS

SUMP-PUMP

Figure 7-1.   Active subslab suction.

nected to the footing drains around the house. If the house has a sump pump installed to reduce water infiltration, a **sump-hole suction system** can be installed by capping the sump hole and at-taching a pipe and fan to it. Often used with subslab suction, **block-wall suction** can be used to remove radon from the interior of the hollow concrete blocks in the foundation.

If the house has a crawlspace, radon can be reduced by venti-lating it with or without a fan (the former being more effective). Crawlspace ventilation reduces the suction effect caused by warm air rising within the home. Another technique used in crawlspaces is **submembrane depressurization,** which simply means covering the earth floor with a plastic membrane and us-ing a pipe and fan to suck the radon from under the sheet to be vented.

Another good idea is to reverse the process by blowing air **into** the basement or lower level while leaving vent windows open to prevent radon from rising into other levels of the house. A **heat-recovery ventilator** (HRV), also known as an **air-to-air heat ex-**

changer, can be installed, which will increase ventilation while using heated or cooled air that is exhausted toward the warm or cool incoming air.

In general, it's a good idea to remedy the problem from the beginning by having the house tested for radon before you buy it and making the test a requirement of your purchase offer. If radon is present, you may be able to negotiate all or part of the repair cost with the owner.

How to Find and Eliminate Radon in the Water

If you are interested in a home that has water supplied by a private well, you should contact either a local laboratory that is qualified to test for radon in water or call the EPA Drinking Water Hotline at (800) 426-4791 for more information. Another way to test for radon in the water is to use continuous-radon monitors such as the EPAA86b or EPA87b. These monitors measure radon concentrations in a closed bathroom before and after the hot water runs for more than 10 minutes. If the water contains more than 40,000 pCi/l of radon, it may be contributing a significant amount of radon to the air inside the house. According to the EPA, there is no documented evidence of a health risk from ingesting radon in drinking water, but breathing radon particles into your lungs is hazardous.

The danger posed by radon in the water is much less than the danger posed by radon gas because the water dilutes the radon and allows it to dissipate. According to the EPA, 10,000 picocuries of radon per liter of water will contribute roughly 1 picocurie of airborne radon to the house air.

If you do find radon in the water, there are two methods you can use to solve the problem. With the **aeration method,** the water can be treated at the well before it enters the house or at the faucet. An aerator tank is installed above the well pump to allow the water to circulate and thus dissipate the gas. A second pump is installed to pump the aerated water into the home. The aerator systems are generally less than 99 percent effective and cost more to install than the **granular activated carbon (GAC) systems,** which are installed on the water line where it enters the house. These systems contain a brand of carbon specifically designed to remove radon, and some of them have been more than

99 percent effective; they are designed to operate for several years. Certain states may require that the contaminated filters be disposed of as low-level radioactive waste products. Check with the local health department in your target area.

Use the following list of phone numbers to contact the EPA office in your state:

Alabama	(800)582-1866
Alaska	(800)478-4845
Arizona	(602)255-4845
Arkansas	(501)661-2301
California	(800)745-7236
Colorado	(800)846-3986
Connecticut	(203)566-3122
Delaware	(800)554-4636
District of Columbia	(202)727-7106
Florida	(800)543-8279
Georgia	(800)745-0037
Guam	(617)646-8863
Hawaii	(808)586-4700
Idaho	(800)445-8647
Illinois	(800)325-1245
Indiana	(800)272-9723
Iowa	(800)383-5992
Kansas	(913)296-1561
Kentucky	(502)564-3700
Louisiana	(800)256-2494
Maine	(800)232-0842
Maryland	(800)872-3666
Massachusetts	(413)586-7525
Michigan	(517)335-8200
Minnesota	(800)798-9050
Mississippi	(800)626-7739
Missouri	(800)669-7236
Montana	(406)444-3671
Nebraska	(800)334-9491
Nevada	(702)687-5394
New Hampshire	(800)852-3345(4674)
New Jersey	(800)648-0394
New Mexico	(505)827-4300

New York	(800)458-1158
North Carolina	(919)571-4141
North Dakota	(701)221-5188
Ohio	(800)523-4439
Oklahoma	(405)271-5221
Oregon	(503)731-4014
Pennsylvania	(800)237-2366
Puerto Rico	(809)767-3563
Rhode Island	(401)277-2438
South Carolina	(800)768-0362
South Dakota	(800)438-3367
Tennessee	(800)232-1139
Texas	(512)834-6688
Utah	(801)536-4250
Vermont	(800)640-0601
Virginia	(800)468-0138
Washington	(800)323-9727
West Virginia	(800)922-1255
Wisconsin	(800)798-9050
Wyoming	(800)458-5847

8

ELECTROMAGNETIC RADIATION

According to the Federal Communications Commission (FCC), **electromagnetic radiation** consists of waves of electric and magnetic energy that move through space. These waves are generated by the *movement* of electrical charges. There are several types of electromagnetic radiation. One type is produced when an alternating electrical current (AC) creates waves that emanate from a radio antenna; these waves are called **radio frequency (RF) radiation.**

Electromagnetic waves travel at the speed of light, and each wave is associated with a wavelength and frequency that is related to a simple mathematical formula: frequency × wavelength = speed of light. High-frequency waves have short wavelengths, and low-frequency waves have long wavelengths. Electrical power is extremely low frequency (ELF) radiation, and X rays and gamma rays have very high frequencies. In between these extremes lie radio waves, microwaves, infrared radiation, visible light, and ultraviolet light.

Electromagnetic radiation is measured in frequencies from about 3 kilohertz to 300 gigahertz. One **hertz** (Hz) equals one cycle per second; a kilohertz (kHz) is 1,000 hertz, a megahertz

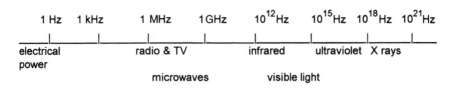

Figure 8-1. The electromagnetic spectrum.

(MHz) is 1 million hertz, and a gigahertz (GHz) is 1 billion hertz. Figure 8-1 will give you an idea of the power requirements of the various forms of radiation.

Another form of radiation that is of concern to the general public is microwave radiation. We use microwave radiation not only to cook our food but also to communicate by means of microwave relay antennas. You should be concerned if your home is located in the vicinity of either high-powered electrical transmission lines or a microwave transmission tower.

The potential health threat posed by close exposure to microwave radiation is that it produces heat in the body by means of a resonant effect caused by sound waves, which is the same principle used to heat food in a microwave oven. If the body does not have the capacity to dissipate the heat, damage can occur. This is known as the **thermal effect.**

The levels of microwave radiation encountered by the general public are far below the levels required to cause tissue damage. However, the **calcium-influx effect**—the sped-up release of calcium ions from animal brain tissue—has been observed at levels well below those necessary to produce heat or tissue damage.

There is much controversy over how much exposure to these forms of radiation is safe. In the United States there are emission standards for items like microwave ovens, but there are no official federal standards relating to the long-range effects of exposure to low levels of radiation. Because this subject is so controversial, if you are interested in a home in an area that has high-power lines or microwave transmission towers nearby, you can receive more information by contacting the EPA's Office of Radiation and Indoor Air at (202) 260-7751. If anyone in your family needs an electrical device for medical reasons such as a cardiac pacemaker, you should definitely contact the EPA before you make your final decision. I also recommend calling the local power company and asking them to test the area; then have an independent test done by an impartial party and compare the two sets of results.

The most controversial form of electromagnetic radiation is produced in the high-power electric lines that crisscross the country. The high voltage that runs through these lines creates an electromagnetic field that is considered nonionizing, which means they do not excite the molecules of air that are near them as a microwave oven does.

Electric fields are produced by the presence of electricity, and magnetic fields are produced by the movement of electricity. Remember in high school, when iron filings were shaken onto a piece of paper and a magnet was held under the paper creating lines of magnetic force? EMFs work the same way, with lines of electromagnetic force radiating out from the power source. Since 1979, studies of the effects of **electromagnetic fields (EMFs)** on the human population suggest that exposure to EMFs may be linked to certain types of cancer, but to date there is no positive proof to support this belief.

The unit of measurement for EMFs is known as a *gauss.* The intensity of the magnetic field is measured in thousandths of a gauss, or milligauss (mG).

Every electrical wire and appliance produces an electromagnetic field. The electromagnetic field of the earth is measured at 500 milligauss. To give you a better idea of the range of exposure to EMFs in our daily life, the list in Table 8.1 rates the highest readings for a variety of common household appliances.

As you can see from Table 8.1, the closer you are to an electrical appliance, the higher your exposure is to the electromagnetic field created by the appliance. Can openers create the largest field of EMF radiation, and the coffee makers create the smallest. And there's a valid reason not to use that vacuum cleaner too often.

Now that you're familiar with the EMF exposure to which you're subjected by your everyday appliances, let's look at Table 8.2 to see how much radiation the power lines near our homes produce. Remember that when you stand under a power line, you are already 20 feet away from it, depending on the average height of the line. Under a typical 230-kilovolt (kV) power line, the magnetic field is probably less than 120 milligauss.

Table 8.1. Milligauss Readings of Household Appliances

	Distance from Source			
	6 Inches	1 Foot	2 Feet	4 Feet
Hair dryer	700	70	10	1
Electric shaver	600	100	10	1
Coffee maker	10	1	—	—
Dishwasher	100	30	7	1
Food processor	130	20	3	—
Can opener	1,500	300	30	4
Microwave oven	300	200	30	20
Electric range	200	30	9	6
Toaster	20	7	—	—
Color TV	N/A	20	8	4
Vacuum cleaner	700	200	50	10
Iron	20	3	—	—

Table 8.2. Milligauss Readings of High-Voltage Power Lines

	Distance from Lines			
Type of Transmission Lines	50 Feet	100 Feet	200 Feet	300 Feet
115 Kilovolt, average usage	7	2	0.4	0.2
115 Kilovolt, peak usage	14	4	0.9	0.4
230 Kilovolt, average usage	20	7	1.8	0.8
230 Kilovolt, peak usage	40	15	3.6	1.6
500 Kilovolt, average usage	29	13	3.2	1.4
500 Kilovolt, peak usage	62	27	6.7	3.0

There are presently no federal or state regulations or guide-
lines about EMFs relating to real estate transactions. New York
State currently allows an exposure of 200 milligauss at the edge
of power line rights-of-way (see chapter 10). You will have to
judge whether or not you feel comfortable with it. There is not
enough information regarding EMFs to be able to definitely state
that they are harmful, but I try to stay away from anything that
makes my car radio sound like static hash.

In addition to the potential physical harm that can come from
prolonged exposure to this type of radiation, you need to judge

the effects of close proximity to high-voltage power lines on the value of a home. My experience has been that if a building lot or a home is within about a quarter-mile radius of a high-power line that is situated so that the owner would be reminded of its presence every day, the property usually will sell for a lower price than it would otherwise. But I have seen many homes in close proximity to high-power lines sold to people who just don't take it as a serious threat. It simply boils down to personal preference and often affordability.

Personally, if I drive near or under a power line that makes my radio sound like two dozen frying eggs, I have to wonder what that will do to my brain over a prolonged period. Heck, I wonder what it does to me as I'm driving under it.

If you have concerns about locating near an electromagnetic source, contact the EPA office in your area and obtain all the information they have on this type of radiation. There are several ways to test your existing or future home with certain devices sensitive to EMFs.

9

WATER—WHERE DOES IT COME FROM?

Outside of the areas whose population demands the necessity of central water and sewer systems, people must use a well and septic system. In Figure 9-1 you see a more modern representation of the old well with the hand pump. In the old days, wells were dug by hand, and the top of the well was sealed to make it airtight. The hand pump was installed with a pipe extended into the water. Suction provided by pumping the handle brought water to the surface. The well shown in Figure 9-1 was drilled through the soil and into the bedrock. A collection cylinder with a weep hole was installed below the frost line to allow water to leak (weep) into the collection cylinder and be pumped to the surface. Another way to collect water was to build a large tank or cistern out of either wood or metal and put it in the attic to collect rainwater. The weight of the water in the cistern provided enough pressure to force the water down through the pipes and faucets.

Although municipal water systems are convenient, they obtain their water from either reservoirs (lakes or rivers) or their own drilled-well systems. Consider where that water comes from. If the water comes from reservoirs, it is exposed to various

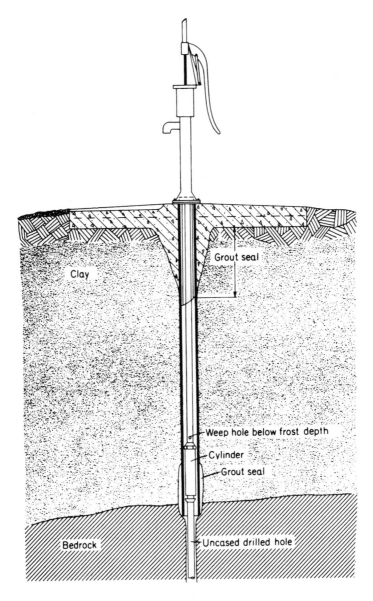

Figure 9-1. Hand-pump well.

sources of contamination. Have you ever gone fishing at the reservoir? Are people boating and swimming in it? Two other examples of sources of contamination are acid rain and surface runoff from land surrounding the reservoir.

To combat contamination of municipal water supplies, the water must be treated with chemicals to kill bacteria and viruses. According to information provided by the New York State Department of Health, Bureau of Water Supply Protection, a number of chemicals can be used. Chlorine appears to be the most popular in the Northeast. Iodine can also be used. Other chemicals can be used for other purposes, such as calcium carbonate to inhibit corrosion of the water system.

If I were to mention all the chemical processes available to clean up water, you might go running to the nearest water softener company screaming to save your children from becoming chemically altered mutant monsters. There is no reason to be afraid of these chemicals as far as I know. Millions of people use these systems throughout the country, with not only state regulations to abide by but stringent federal regulations as well. Besides that, each county, town, and city has its own standards thrown in to the regulatory soup solely for your protection. I have lived with both municipal and well water, and my personal preference is natural well water.

One of the major complaints with municipal water is its **turbidity,** or lack of clarity. I was never comfortable drawing water from the tap and raising it to my lips only to see particles of *something* floating towards the bottom. I realized that what I was seeing was only coagulated minerals, dissolved calcium and magnesium bicarbonates, or simple natural elements reacting to the chemical treatments. But to me it was *something* floating in my water.

Because bacterial contamination was eliminated by the municipality with chlorine, I had a water filter installed using activated charcoal with a reverse-osmosis system to remove the floaters in my water. This removed both the floaters and the odor from the chemical treatment, and now my water is crystal clear.

Ground water drawn from a well system must also be treated if it is used in a municipal system. Water will cleanse itself by percolation through the soil and into the water table. Ground water is normally not subject to animal, human, or runoff contamina-

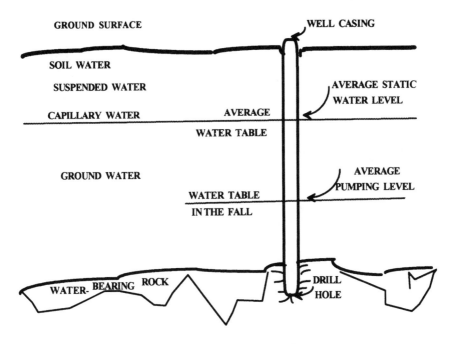

Figure 9-2.   Water levels.

tion. Remember the difference between surface water and ground water? Look at Figure 9-2 to see the different levels of water.

Just below the surface you see **soil water** and then **suspended water.** Both of these are considered surface water. Below the suspended water is the capillary water, where the surface water interacts with the ground water. Notice the two levels of the water table: the **average water table** and the **fall water table.** Below the ground water level, you see **water-bearing rock,** with crevices and fissures to allow the ground water to seep into the hole left by the drilled well. This illustration is a typical cross-section of the northeast part of the United States. In other areas of the country, the rock may be much closer to the surface, or the water table itself may be much lower or even nonexistent.

Take a look at Figure 9-3, which shows three typical drilled wells. Note the appearance of the well caps, the tops of the wells that protrude above the ground. You will see three types of pump systems with pipes going through the foundation to the well's storage tank or pressure tank. The most widely used pump in the

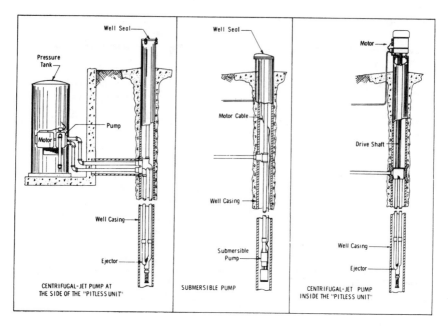

Figure 9-3.   Drilled wells.

Northeast is the **submersible pump,** in which the well pump is
located near the bottom of the well. With the **centrifugal (side) jet
pump,** the well pump is located either on or near the storage tank
or higher in the well casing. With the (inside) centrifugal well,
the motor is mounted at the top of the casing with the pump located at the pitless adapter where the water intake line to the
house joins the well. Drilled wells with a submersible pump are
the most popular; with these, a hole is drilled into the soil with
a diameter of six to eight inches and a depth of anywhere from 50
to more than 200 feet.

As the well is drilled, a casing made of steel is lowered into
the well to keep its sides from caving in. Concrete may be used
on the outside of the casing to seal the well from intrusion of
contaminated surface water. The pump is lowered into the well
to a foot or so above the bottom of the hole. The well should be
pumped for a full 24 hours, and a well log should be maintained
to ensure that the well can produce a minimum of five gallons
per minute over a 24-hour period. Five gallons per minute may
not sound like much but remember, that's **per minute.** Multiply

five gallons per minute by 60 minutes per hour and again by 24 hours in a day, and you'll see that this well can produce 7,200 gallons of water per day. In addition to the production of new water, there is the storage capacity of the water in the well casing itself. A casing with a diameter of six inches and a depth of 20 feet should have a storage capacity of 1.47 gallons per foot of casing, or 29.4 gallons stored at any time in the well casing. If the casing extends to 200 feet, you can have almost 300 gallons of water stored in the casing alone.

With this well we may be producing a lot of water, but how much do we use every day? Look at the chart in Table 9.1 to get an idea of how much water is used during the course of an average day. The numbers in the column on the right reflect how many gallons of water are used each time you use one of the items listed on the left. Add up how many times you use the toilet, bathroom sink, shower, and so on, on a daily basis. Multiply that number by the number of people in your family who also use those facilities. The average usage is between 75 to 150 gallons per day per person in each household. (Although children are smaller, they use more water for washing and baths.) If you have five people in your family, your household can use more than 1,500 gallons of water per day, well within the limits of our five-gallon-per minute well.

When you add up the amount of water we use on an annual basis, it amounts to a tremendous volume that we all take for granted. If we are going to save this earth, we all must try to change the way we use our natural resources. One way to conserve water—and, if you are hooked into a municipal water system, to save money—is to use certain water-saving devices that

Table 9.1. Miscellaneous Water Use Estimates (in Gallons)

Toilet	4 to 6 per use
Bathroom sink	1 to 1.2 per use
Bathtub	30 per use
Shower	25 to 30 per use
Dishwasher	9.5 to 15.5 per load
Clothes washer	25 to 50 per load
Lawn sprinkler	120 per hour
3,000-sq.-ft. lawn, watered 1 inch per week	1,850 per week

limit the amount of water flowing from the shower head and bath and kitchen sinks. Most of these involve an aerator with small holes in it; the holes actually increase the pressure at the nozzle, and because the holes are quite small, you use less water to do the same job. You can also add inserts to the toilet tank to reduce the amount of water needed to flush. There are also a variety of water-saving toilets on the market that will pay for themselves over time. By using these devices you can save money or reduce the flow of moisture into your septic system that it has to process, especially in periods of excessive rain or snow melt when the septic system may become saturated by surface water.

In older (pre-1960) homes you will find a different type of well called a **point well** or **driven well,** in which a point (1.5 to 2 inches in diameter) is driven into the ground by a hand maul or drive shoe. Point wells are usually shallow and feed from surface water. Figure 9-4 shows the difference between a driven well and a point well. You cannot see a **point well** when you are inspecting a home, but you'll know that there's one on the property by the presence of the pump and storage tank.

Figure 9-5 is a typical example of a pump motor and storage tank for a point well. A point well should be either inside the home or inside an attached structure to minimize the possibility of surface water entering the well. There may or may not be a manhole to the surface if the well is underground. I have seen the well pump and storage tanks located under a porch. Because most point wells require an enclosure, you will probably find the well very near or in the house, whereas a drilled well can be located anywhere.

Occasionally the point well will be located inside the main level of the home, in an attached structure, or in the basement like the one shown in Figure 9.5. If the setup looks like that, chances are it is a point well. Remember, point wells are normally shallow, and you should ascertain how deep the well point is. In periods of dry weather or droughts, a point well may not be deep enough, and the water table may fall below the level of the well.

If the home is connected to a central or municipal water supply and has been vacant for several weeks or more, it is a good idea to open all faucets and allow fresh water to drain the old standing water out of the system for at least 15 to 20 minutes. If

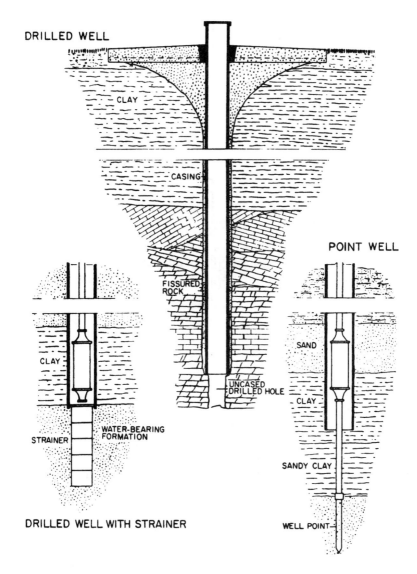

DRILLED WELL

CLAY

CASING

POINT WELL

FISSURED ROCK

SAND

CLAY

CLAY

UNCASED DRILLED HOLE

WATER-BEARING FORMATION

STRAINER

SANDY CLAY

DRILLED WELL WITH STRAINER

WELL POINT

Figure 9-4.   Drilled and point wells.

the home is serviced by a well and has been vacant for several weeks or more, include in your purchase offer a requirement that the well water be tested for contamination by an independent laboratory. The most popular water test is the Total Coliform Bacteria test. If you are located in a farm area, you should

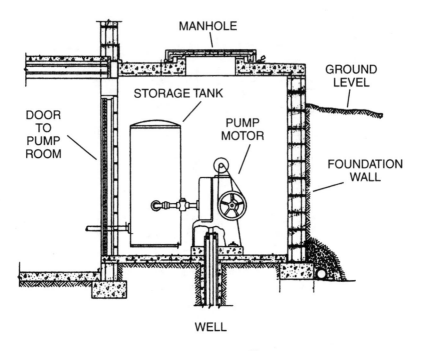

MANHOLE

GROUND LEVEL

STORAGE TANK

DOOR TO PUMP ROOM

PUMP MOTOR

FOUNDATION WALL

WELL

Figure 9-5.   Point well motor.

also test for various herbicides and pesticides to be sure they have not leached into the water table. If you are near a landfill, test for organic material; if you are near an industrial site, test for chemicals or heavy metals; if you are near gasoline storage, test for petrochemicals. For more information, contact the local, state, or county health department. If there is a problem, the owner should resolve it for you before selling the property. Usually, chlorine is used to decontaminate, or **shock,** the well. The chlorine is mixed with water and pumped through the pipes in the house and is also poured into the well itself and left standing for at least eight hours. When all the chlorine is pumped out, the water should be retested, and the contamination should be gone.

I prefer well water. I can live with and resolve any problems with mineral content. Another thing I like about a well is the only cost for my water is the electricity to run the pump, which is much less than the cost of buying water from the municipality.

HOW DO I FIND THE WELL?

If you have access to the survey for the lot (see the next chapter), you should be able to see where the well is. The well should be identified by a small circle with a W next to it. If the survey does not show the well location or there is no survey available, you have to go hunting.

If the well was installed after the early 1970s, you should see a well cap (seal) protruding about six inches above the ground (refer to Figure 9-3). The well cap may be plastic or metal and looks like an inverted soup bowl. Before the early 1970s, most well caps were buried just under the surface of the ground, and you may require a metal detector to find them.

If the house has a basement or full foundation, you should be able to pinpoint the general location of the well by locating the inlet of the water pipe and electric lines that pass through the foundation.

If the well is buried and no one knows where it is, you may have to dig up the water line, starting from the foundation, to be sure of where it is. If you have a general idea where the well is, a metal detector may allow you to locate it without digging up the yard.

Regardless of where the well is located, it should not be any closer than 100 feet to the septic absorption fields if the lot is level or the well is higher in elevation than the septic system. If the well is at a lower elevation than the septic system, then there should be at least 200 feet from the outside edge of the septic fields to the well cap. The last thing you want is the effluent from the septic fields draining into your well water. If you have enough separation between the well and septic system and the proper elevation (the well cap higher than the septic system), then there should be no danger from the septic system effluent reaching the ground water that feeds the well.

HOW DOES A SEPTIC SYSTEM WORK?

If your target home is connected to a central or municipal sewer system, you don't have much to do but try not to plug the drains during the course of your daily life. However, you will have to pay a fee to use the system. If the home is serviced by a **septic system** or **on-site wastewater disposal system,** as millions of homes are, you should know something about how they are built and how they work to keep your investment worry free.

According to *Onsite Disposal Systems,* a manual made available by the Environmental Protection Agency, in 1980 approximately 18 million housing units disposed of their wastewater using some form of on-site treatment. That number was expected to grow by one million from 1993 to 1995 due to the shift of the general population from urban to rural areas. If that projected increase was accurate, then roughly 25 million homes were using on-site wastewater treatment in 1995. However, it is estimated that only 32 percent of the total land area in the United States has soils suitable for some type of on-site disposal system.

The privy (Figure 9-6), or outhouse, was a very simple way to dispose of waste before the introduction of indoor plumbing. Most waters that contained grease or soap were emptied onto the ground, and human wastes went into the privy. When the privy pit filled up, which took several years, one simply moved the privy to a new location and covered the hole with soil. I'm sure

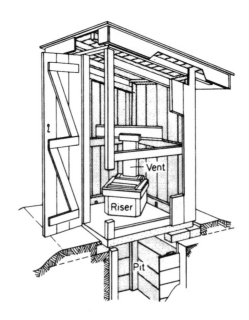

Figure 9-6. Privy.

that in years gone by, some outhouses were not designed as elaborately as the one shown in Figure 9-6.

With more and more people moving from the cities, where municipal water and sewer systems were taken for granted, the problem of waste disposal in the rural areas of the country became more of a concern. Can you imagine a new subdivision, with 100 or more homes with privies in their back yards and a constant stream of people running in and out during the holiday season? How about in the winter?

Because of the influx of new homes being built on lots that were much smaller than those of the older country homes, the septic system was designed. A septic system simply combines waste with air and water in such a way that the waste breaks down in the presence of natural bacteria. The treated **black water** is allowed to flow through a system of pipes to be absorbed by the soil and evaporated into the air. Figure 9-7 shows the layout for a typical septic system. Note the distance of the well from the septic fields.

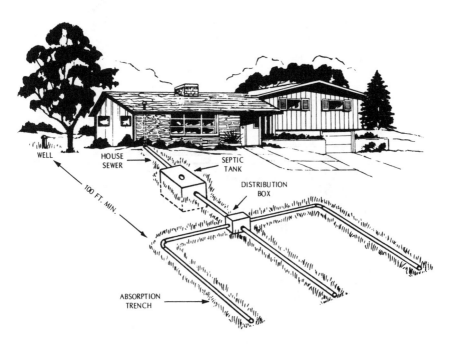

Figure 9-7. A simple septic system.

In order for an on-site wastewater disposal system to work, the soil must be tested to determine its ability to absorb water. A **percolation test (perc)** is performed to this end. The size of the system required is usually determined by a bedroom count, with an average of two people per bedroom, and by the number of bathrooms to be constructed. The number of people expected to use the system and the result of the soil tests determine which type of system will work best and how it should be constructed.

In Figure 9-8 you see two examples of how soil is tested for percolation capabilities. Although this example calls for either a dug hole 12 inches wide or a bored hole 4 inches wide, most towns or counties will allow the hole to be dug with either a shovel or backhoe bucket. The key to the entire process is to measure the amount of time it takes for the soil to absorb 1 inch of water.

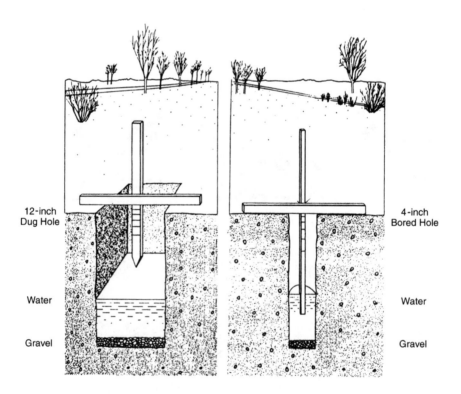

12-inch Dug Hole

Water

Gravel

4-inch Bored Hole

Water

Gravel

Figure 9-8.   Perc test.

To keep it simple, as Figure 9-8 shows, dig or bore a hole about 36 inches deep. Place about 2 inches of gravel in the bottom of the hole. Take a stick or piece of wood lathe and drive a nail through it at a point that will allow the nail to be located about 3 to 5 inches below the top of the hole. Drive another nail through the lathe 1 inch above the first one. Presoak the hole with water several times to simulate rainy conditions and then fill the hole until the water touches the top nail. Note the amount of time it takes for the water to drain down 1 inch to the bottom nail. This test will demonstrate the soil's ability to absorb water. Because rainfall is measured in inches, you have an idea of why this test is performed.

Now that you know how well the first 36 inches of soil absorbs moisture, you have to find out what the soil is like at least five to seven feet down. The actual design of the system will depend not only on the rate of moisture absorption but also on where the effluent from the system is going to go.

As you dig, you may find several different layers of soil. Sometimes the initial layers are a mixture of clay, below which you may find layers of gravel or a combination of soils such as shale, clay, and gravel, or even sand. You don't want the effluent from the septic system to leach into the soil and reach the ground water table before it is cleansed of bacteria, and that takes about five to seven feet of good, drainable soil. The engineer who designs the system must take into account the various types of soil from the surface of the ground to that depth, the slope (topography) of the lot for gravity-fed water flow, the area's climate, the number of people expected to use the system, the location of any adjoining septics and wells in the area, the design and manufacture of the components to be used, and much more. It's not as simple as the privy. There are dozens of on-site disposal system designs to accommodate a variety of soil and lot conditions; Table 9.2 shows some of the minimum requirements for New York State. Each system should be designed by a licensed engineer to give you some protection in the event the system fails due to a design flaw. I have experienced several flawed septic systems that were designed and stamped by a licensed engineer.

The septic system consists of a cast-iron waste line that protrudes under the footing of the home or through the foundation out to the septic tank (see Figure 9-9). A **septic tank** can be built

Table 9.2.   Minimum Septic Tank Requirements in New York

1,2, or 3 bedrooms	1,000 gallon tank
4 bedrooms	1,250 gallon tank
5 bedrooms	1,500 gallon tank
6 bedroom	1,750 gallon tank

out of stones, brick, or concrete blocks. Some of the older tanks were made of steel, but they eventually rusted away over the years. The newer tanks are made of either precast concrete or fiberglass, which is now required by most local health departments.

The effluent flows down the waste line from the house and into the septic tank where it is broken down by bacteria. I like to describe the process as the good guys eating up the bad guys.

Like all microorganisms, bacteria require carbon, nitrogen, phosphorus, sulfur, and other trace elements. They are small chemical factories in which raw materials are processed. Most microorganisms are **heterotrophic,** which means they use organic material for both food and energy. The biochemical process by which the microorganisms convert the waste and use it as energy is known as **metabolism.** The process of matter breaking down into simpler forms is known as **katabolism.**

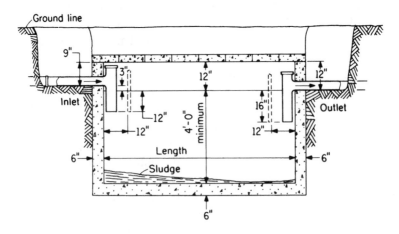

Figure 9-9.   Septic tank.

Organic catalysts (enzymes) are produced by the bacteria to speed up the process of metabolism. Eventually, a constant rate of growth is reached, and the cultures reach a death phase, in which the surviving organisms are fewer than those of the previous generation. Those dead organisms settle to the bottom of the tank as sludge. The constant inflow of new waste material allows the process to continue. Eventually the sludge will accumulate to such an extent that the tank will have to be pumped out. Some experts recommend pumping the tank each year, but that poses the potential problem of removing the microorganisms that are needed for the septic process (the good guys).

Depending on how you use (or abuse) the system, you should be able to use it for several years before you need to pump. Everything that goes into the septic tank must be biodegradable. If you are used to simply flushing everything down the kitchen sink, you will have to change that practice. With a municipal system, people don't have to worry about what is flushed away, but with a septic system, you need to be more careful. You can't simply drain the cooking oil or the leftover pasta into the system. You certainly can't pour paint or solvents into the system. Common sense tells you that anything that will kill you if you drink it will kill the bacteria that your system needs to function. Similarly, if you drink cooking oil, it will clog *your* systems, and it will do the same to the septic system.

Although most health departments require the clothes washer to empty into the septic tank, I do not agree with this practice. Soap, unless it is specifically designed as a biodegradable product, does not break down and forms a film inside the pipes. The soap builds up into a thick scum, plugging the tank, and the tank will have to be pumped.

Contact the local health department and ask for information on the operation of septic systems. They will give you good advice on what should and should not go into the system and will save you aggravation and money in the long run.

I favor the installation of a dry well for the shower and washer water. Many areas do not allow dry wells because of their potential to pollute the surface water and eventually the ground water. A **dry well** is simply a hole dug down about four or five feet deep and filled with rocks or gravel. The shower and washer water (**gray water**) drains into it and eventually into the soil.

If you have a large enough parcel of land, you can locate the dry well far enough away from your well. If the soil is sufficiently permeable, a dry well will not overload your septic system with soapy water. In areas where the lots are smaller and the homes are clustered in a development, dry wells may not be allowed.

There are dozens of septic system designs to accommodate a wide variety of situations. The typical system consists of the septic tank where the waste is naturally treated and a **distribution box** where the effluent flowing from the septic tank is directed to flow into the **septic fields** (also called **absorption fields, leach fields,** or **tile fields**) where the solids can be absorbed into the soil and the moisture is evaporated into the air. The term *tile field* comes from the material that was used in septic systems before the 1960s known as Orangeburg pipe, which was clay tile that was susceptible to breaking or crushing and deteriorated with age. Most systems installed today use a perforated polyvinylchloride (PVC) or plastic pipe that is resistant to crushing and will last for many years. In Figure 9-10 you can see a simple

DISTRIBUTION BOX NETWORK

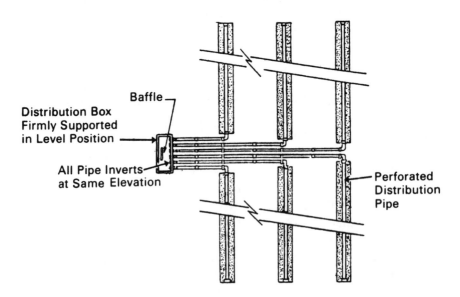

Figure 9-10. Distribution system.

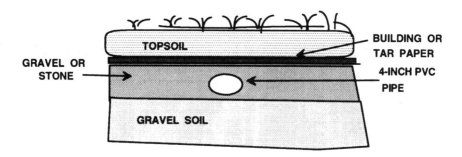

Figure 9-11. Side view of a septic trench.

version of a distribution box and septic field system, and Figure 9-11 shows how the PVC pipe is installed in a trench, surrounded by gravel or washed stone, and covered by building paper or hay.

Although many variables are involved in septic system design, the numbers in Table 9.3 are used in New York State to determine the length of the absorption fields, assuming that the soil is sufficiently permeable. The length is determined by the number of gallons fed into the system per day and the ability of the soil to absorb the moisture based on a perc test. The example in Table 9.3 is based on one to five inches of absorption per minute; this is a great perc rate, but the average perc is more than that. If the soil absorbs the moisture at a slower pace, the size of the tile fields will increase to provide a greater area for evaporation and absorption.

If the lot is flat, you should have a simple septic field system like the one in Figure 9-12; it is called an **in-ground system** be-

Table 9.3. Septic System Sizes

Number of Bedrooms	Gallons per Day	Linear Feet of Pipe
2	200–300	108–125
3	390–450	162–187
4	520–600	216–250
5	650–750	270–312
6	780–900	325–374

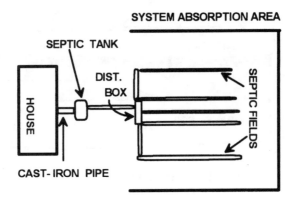

Figure 9-12.   Illustrated septic system.

cause it is installed in the ground. If your lot is on a hillside or has a steep elevation, you can have what is called a **drop-box system,** in which the distribution boxes are set at different levels to follow the elevation of the ground. Another system used for lots that change elevation is the **sloping system,** in which the pipe is installed at different angles to follow the ground's contours.

If the lot has a slow perc or no perc at all, you can still install an **above-ground,** or **fill-section, system** that will work but will be much more expensive than the standard in-ground system. With these systems, you must create an area of good soil where none existed before.

Figures 9-13 and 9-14 show side views of an in-ground and an above-ground system, respectively. The above-ground system is installed in good, permeable soil that was trucked onto the site. The above-ground system is required owing to a higher water

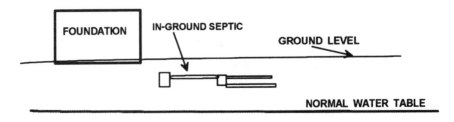

Figure 9-13.   Side view of an in-ground septic system.

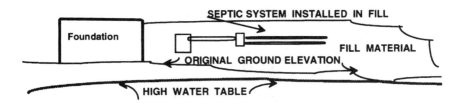

Figure 9-14. Side view of an above-ground septic system.

table and dense clay soil. The perc was very slow, and water was encountered at various depths. There was evidence of outcroppings of rock and shale, which indicate a high elevation of rock throughout the entire parcel.

With an above-ground system (Figure 9-15), you have to create a **berm,** or wall, out of impermeable clay. The berm must be several feet high, wider at the base, and narrow at the top. It forms a four-sided enclosure like a swimming pool into which you put a good, moisture-absorbent soil such as bank-run gravel to a depth of one to five feet, as seen in Figure 9-16. The soil must be allowed to settle or else should be mechanically compacted every six inches. You will need a much larger area of ground to build this type of septic system because you are creating what Mother Nature didn't give you. You must set the system far enough away from the edge of the lot to meet the health department's requirements. Fill-section systems usually require more linear feet of pipe to allow for an even greater area of absorption and evaporation.

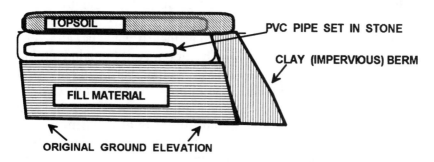

Figure 9-15. Cutaway side view of an above-ground septic system.

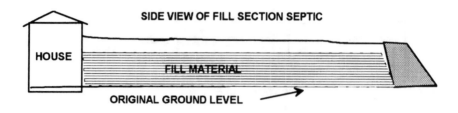

SIDE VIEW OF FILL SECTION SEPTIC

HOUSE

FILL MATERIAL

ORIGINAL GROUND LEVEL

TOP VIEW OF FILL SECTION SEPTIC

BERM MATERIAL

FILL MATERIAL

**Figure 9-16.   Long side and top view of a fill-section septic system
with berm material.**

A simple in-ground system may cost anywhere from $1,500 to
$3,000, depending on the area, but a fill-section system will usu-
ally cost about three to five times that amount because you have
to purchase and install the fill material. Here's how I figured out
the total cost of a fill-section system I had to build. The area to be
filled with gravel was 40 feet wide by 60 feet long by 4 feet deep—
a total of 9,600 cubic feet. Dividing 9,600 by 27 to obtain the cubic yardage yields 355, and adding 10 percent of 355 to allow for
settling of the fill material gave me 390.5 cubic yards, which I
rounded up to 391 cubic yards. At the time, bank-run gravel cost
$7.50 per cubic yard, so that's $2,932.50 just for the gravel. The
berm had two sides that were 40 feet long and two sides that were
60 feet long, which equals 200 linear feet. It was also an average
of 12 feet wide and four feet high, which meant I needed a total of
9,600 cubic feet, or approximately 355 cubic yards, of clay. Good,
impermeable clay sold for $12 per cubic yard, so that was another
$4,260 to be spent on the system. Then I estimated that installing
all this material would take about 30 hours of machine time, or
another $1,800. Because the septic fields were fairly large, the ac-
tual system components cost $4,000, so the final grand total was
$12,992.50. Pretty expensive, huh?

If the lot is such that the system can be installed at an elevation that will allow for effluent to be gravity-fed from the septic tank to the absorption field, then the above-ground system will fit nicely. If the lot is level, you will see a large hill of earth (the berm and the above-ground system) and a valley between the house and the system, with the sewer pipe suspended in the air. Now you must buy additional fill material for that area between the system and the house (see Figure 9-17).

You can identify an above-ground system by looking at the lot. If you see a small hill or mound (a **mound system** is another type of above-ground system) higher than the surrounding ground, it is very possible that the septic system may be of the fill-section variety.

One drawback to an above-ground system is that over time, if the system is not used properly and oils and other materials that don't belong in the system infiltrate it, the fill material will eventually become saturated. If that happens, the fill material will have to be removed, and new material will have to be installed at great expense.

Chances are that you will be buying a home that already has a septic system installed and you don't have to worry about building it; however, you must make sure that the existing system is functioning well before you buy. One good way is to perform a dye test. If you hire a house inspector, he or she will do the test; if you don't hire an inspector, contact the local health department for instructions. You can buy the dye at a local hardware store, but be careful—this stuff will not come out of your clothes and will stain your skin if you spill it (I know this from personal experience). You put the dye into a toilet and flush it down (wait until the next day if the system is still being used). In a vacant house, you may have to flush the toilet several times. If the

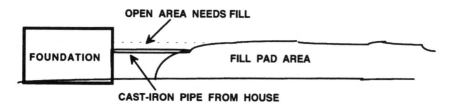

Figure 9-17. Additional fill requirements.

system is leaking, you should see the dye leak out somewhere in the yard. If you don't see the dye, the system may be working properly.

For lots whose small size will not allow for an absorption field, you may be able to use a **leaching-tank system.** Like a septic tank, a leaching-tank system can be built out of rock, bricks, concrete blocks, or precast concrete.

Check Figure 9-18 for a side view of a leaching-tank system. These systems can only be used in areas of good, gravelly soil. The leaching-tank replaces the septic field and acts almost like another septic tank except that it has holes to allow the effluent to leach into the surrounding soil. You will install several tanks that, when calculated for size and soil type, will actually process the same amount of effluent as the septic-field system. They work great for small lots, but as I said, the soil must be gravelly, and you may need access to a municipal water system. If the lot is small, you may not be able to meet the separation requirements (see chapters 10 on surveys and 11 on zoning) between your septic system, your well, and the surrounding wells and septic systems. You don't want to drink the water from the ground if the area has a high concentration of small lots with septic systems.

It is very important that you find the boundaries of the septic system. The last thing you want to do is to build that new in-ground swimming pool in the middle of your septic fields.

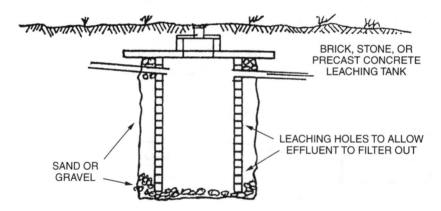

Figure 9-18.   A leaching-tank system.

The septic system works on the principles of absorption and evaporation, which means you shouldn't plant trees to block the sun in that area. In fact, you shouldn't plant anything in or near the system. Certain plants, like the weeping willow tree, have a great propensity for water, and if they grow near a septic system, they will drive their roots into the leach pipes and plug the system. You should also locate the septic tank and mark it with a rock or stake. You may need to pump the tank in the future, and you won't want to dig up half the yard to find it. Also, don't drive over the system with your car or truck. Although the PVC pipes are strong, you can knock them out of alignment or the distribution box out of a level position, and then you will have another problem; if the pipes are clay, you will crush them.

Plant grass on it, play on it, walk on it and sit on it—that's it. If you are careful, you should be able to enjoy many years of problem-free use of your septic system without paying the local sewer company for the privilege.

10

WHAT IS A SURVEY?

A survey performed on a parcel of land will determine the exact boundaries of that parcel, not only in relation to adjoining properties but also in relation to other parcels on all sides of the surveyed parcel, whether they abut the surveyed parcel or not. The survey determines where the parcel lies within a certain area and how the parcel is oriented in each direction, north, south, east, and west. The survey measures the boundaries in linear feet and actually locates the parcel on the earth by using longitude and latitude. The survey should be performed by a licensed surveyor. A surveyor is **not** an engineer, although sometimes the two are confused. The surveyor determines the location and orientation of a property; the engineer designs whatever is needed to make the property usable. Occasionally you will find one individual who is licensed as both a surveyor and an engineer, but normally each is a separate profession.

In prior years, owners measured their property with a set of chains that were of a determined length. One surveyor's chain measured 66 feet in length, or 20.1168 meters. The chains were further broken down by links. One surveyor's link measured 7.92 inches, or 0.201 meters. Another device used was the rod, which measured 16.5 feet or 5.5 yards. If you look up old deeds in the county records, you will find descriptions that read "so many rods, so many chains, and so many links." The length and width of a parcel was determined by adding the chains, rods, and links on all sides of the parcel. Nowadays in the United States, we use linear feet and inches (so far) and convert them to square feet to determine the size of a parcel of land. Land is also measured in acres. One **acre** equals 43,560 square feet. This is also known as a **long acre,** which, just to confuse you, measures 160 square rods. To keep the numbers simple when calculating property sizes and formulating zoning laws, city, town, and county planners decided to round the long acre to the **short acre,** which measures 40,000 square feet. A lot that is 200 feet wide and 200 feet long measures one short acre in area. To keep it simple, if one short acre is 40,000 square feet, then a half acre must be about 20,000 square feet and a quarter acre must be about 10,000 square feet.

By the same token, one-third of an acre is about 13,000 square feet. If you see a property with 100 feet of **frontage,** which is that portion of the property that fronts on the road, and the property is about 130 feet deep, then the entire parcel is about that size. Simply multiply the width (the measurement of the road frontage) by the depth (the measurement from front to back) to estimate the size of the lot. This is easy if the lot is a perfect square or rectangle, but very few properties have exact dimensions.

These calculations will give you a close approximation of the property's size, but an actual survey will give you the exact size and dimensions, and that is one reason it is needed. The surveyor will measure all sides of the parcel in feet and inches, making allowance for oddly shaped or zigzag property lines, and calculate its overall area in square feet. When the survey is completed, you will know the actual and precise size of the parcel and its location on the planet by longitude and latitude. The surveyor will place that information on the survey and draw up a separate written description known as the **deed description,** also known as the **metes and bounds description** (see the example of a Bargain and Sale deed in chapter 13).

The deed description should exactly match the information on the survey. The title attorney will check both documents to make sure they coincide. If they do not match (because deed descriptions usually remain the same from sale to sale and all of the former deeds are recorded in the county records), the survey is considered **open.** The surveyor will have to reevaluate his calculations, refer to the former deeds, and ascertain if any changes were made to the property lines. If no changes were made, the survey should **close,** or continue along the original lot lines. If changes were made, those changes should have received municipal approval and should be recorded in the county records.

By incorporating any changes into the new deed description, the surveyor should be able to close the survey and satisfy the title company. The deed description will be placed on your deed. Your **deed is your title** to the property. Figure 10-1 is a representation of the actual survey of one of my own properties.

The diamond with the S in it in Figure 10-1 is the proposed septic field location; just behind that is the proposed house and driveway location, and far to the back is the proposed well location. Oddly enough, although the lot's elevation drops down from the road as you walk further into the property, the septic system must be located on the front of the lot near the road. Why not put the septic system in the rear (lower) area, you ask? Good question! The septic system must be at least 100 feet from any wells, that's why. If the soil on this lot was not beautiful bank-run gravel, it would be undevelopable until a central sewer was installed because there is not enough room to install an above-ground system. Luckily the soil is excellent, and an in-ground system will fit on the front of the lot. To compensate for the higher elevation of the system, we will build the house even higher to allow for waste to be gravity-fed into the system. We

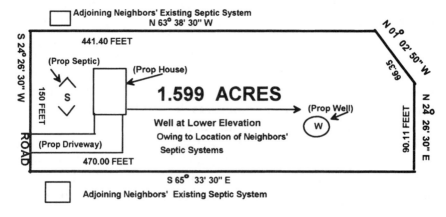

Figure 10-1.   Survey example.

can design the house to have the garage underneath it in a split-level or bi-level style. We can leave the back of the foundation wall exposed and install sliding glass doors so that the basement can be used as living space, enabling the inhabitants to walk out to the lower (ground) level in the back of the house.

As I said before, every lot tells a story, and you must be able to read that story to be able to use the lot in the best way.

The survey will also show the location of the well or water line, septic system or sewer line, driveway, and any other **outbuildings** such as an attached garage or barn. If there are any other items on the parcel such as a fence or stone wall, they should be on the survey also. You want to see everything to which you claim ownership on the survey. The surveyor should be licensed and should certify the survey with his or her official stamp and signature when it is finished. If there is a dispute, possibly with an adjoining neighbor, as to where the lot lines actually are, you can refer to the certified survey and contact the surveyor to verify it. Because the survey has been certified, you may have a legal claim against the surveyor in the event a mistake has been made. Before the bank will commit to a closing date, it will require a copy of the certified survey to show that everything it is lending against is truly there and within the property lines. The title company will also want a copy. The survey will have to be certified to the bank, to the title company, to you, and to the town if a certificate of occupancy (c-of-o) is required because the home is new. A c-of-o may also be required by the lender even if the house is old and predates the town ordinances, in which case you may have to have the house checked out by the building inspector. This holds true for any additions that were constructed after the original was built, which is another reason to have the survey updated. If an addition was built after the original c-of-o and a new c-of-o was not obtained for the addition, then that addition is illegal. If the additions do not show on the old survey, the lender and the title company will not allow the loan to close title.

Sometimes, especially if the house predates the town building codes and was built when the area was not crowded and there was plenty of vacant land around the lot, the original owners didn't pay much attention to how much land they cleared over the years and sometimes built new driveways and storage sheds over the lot lines (boundary lines) (see Figure 10-2). Eventually

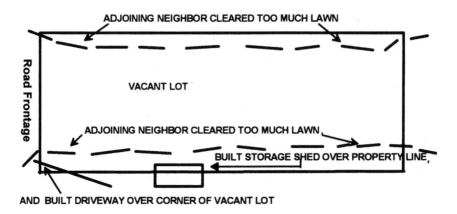

Figure 10-2. Encroaching neighbors.

someone else buys the house, the lender accepts the old survey because it did not change, and everyone is happy—until someone buys the adjacent lot. This person has a survey done and finds that the former owner of the old, adjacent house built his driveway over the corner of the vacant lot or built a storage shed over the property line. This is not an unusual situation; I have experienced it many times when buying building lots in older subdivisions or **scattered lots.**

When someone builds over the line, it is called an **encroachment** onto someone else's property. This encroachment creates **a cloud on title.** The title is not clear because there is an encroachment onto the lot. By definition, an encroachment is something permanent, such as a driveway or an actual outbuilding. If the land was simply cleared for more lawn, there is no encroachment unless the existing owner claims rights to the land, and he or she would have no rights to it unless ownership could be proven by certified survey. Certain states allow **squatters rights,** which means that if someone maintains a property and pays taxes on it for from five to seven years without a challenge from the original owner, then that person may claim ownership of that property.

If you are buying an older home, ask if the survey has been updated, if any additions were built after the original structure was built, and if any c-of-o was issued for the original house and any additions. You should also ask to see a copy of the survey. Verify that everything you are buying lies within the lot's property lines. If there is an encroachment, the matter must be settled before the lender will close the loan.

I purchased a building lot in the late 1970s in a good area of East Fishkill, New York. The lot was relatively level and wooded, and the soil tested out OK. However, the survey showed that the adjoining neighbor had rebuilt his driveway and built a concrete retaining wall at the end of the driveway—no problem, except that the retaining wall was on my lot and was definitely a permanent structure. I asked the owner if he would be willing to move the retaining wall. He was an elderly man and explained that it would be very expensive and would ruin his driveway. I must admit, it did look nice. I could have demanded that the wall be removed and he would have had to remove it, or I could have demanded that he buy that small portion of the lot. This would have required planning board approval to subdivide out that small portion of land; it would have been time consuming and very expensive.

He was a nice guy, and it did look nice, so what to do? I had to satisfy the title company, which had to satisfy the bank to be able to finance the new house. I could not receive clear title with the retaining wall encroaching on my land.

I asked the title company if they would insure the title if the neighbor signed an affidavit binding on his **heirs and assigns,** meaning binding on anyone to whom he wills or sells the property, that if any owner of my lot at any time in the future required the retaining wall to be removed, my neighbor or his heirs and assigns would have to do it. The title company said that if the neighbor were to file a new deed with that requirement (making the requirement a **deed restriction**), they would allow it. That's what we did. A deed restriction remains with the deed no matter who owns the property, and whoever accepts title to the property accepts responsibility for the restriction. You may find deed restrictions created by the original developer that limit the size of house that can be built so as to maintain the property values in the subdivision.

Other deed restrictions may specify that the property can never be further subdivided. You can place almost anything in the deed as a restriction as long as it does not violate existing laws. A deed restriction will apply from the time it is inserted in the deed unless someone at some time challenges it in court and is allowed to nullify the restriction, which is a difficult thing to do.

The moral of this story is that although there was a problem, I was able to handle it to everyone's satisfaction without a big hassle and lawsuits flying around, and I achieved my original objective, which was to buy the lot, build a new house, and sell it for profit. If you have a problem with a survey or neighbor, see if you can resolve the problem as simply as possible. Remember the KISS theory. If you cannot resolve the problem in a nice way, you can always call an attorney and fight it out, but trying the simple way first will save you time, money, and aggravation.

WHAT IS ELEVATION?

Earlier, I described how one of my building lots dropped down to a lower elevation as you walked from the front of the lot toward the rear. It is important to be able to understand the lay of the land, not only the size of the parcel or the dimensions of the lot lines but also the various elevations of the land. Certain areas of the land will be higher or lower. When you try to figure out the best place on the lot to locate the septic system or the house, you have to know where the lowest points are so that the septic system can be gravity-fed and water will not drain into your foundation when it rains. It is also important to be familiar with the topography of the lot to figure out which style of house should be built on it (see Figure 10-3).

Try to imagine building a one-story ranch house with the garage in the basement. If the lot were level, you would have to drive down into a hole in the ground to reach the garage level. A garage-under house is less expensive to build than a house and separate garage because the garage is incorporated into the main structure of the house; otherwise, you are actually building another small house. Of course, a garage wouldn't need heat, water, sewers, tile or carpet, and trim or molding material, but the actual structure is where the most money is spent for labor and materials. If the house is built in the slab-up style, you can incorporate the garage into the first floor, but you can't build a garage-under house on a flat lot unless the garage is part of the first floor at ground level.

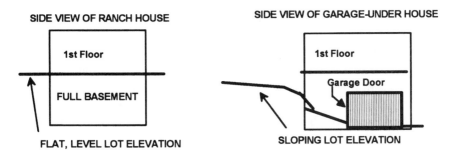

Figure 10-3. Different elevations allow for different styles of home.

To determine which style of home is best suited for your lot, you have to check the lot's width and depth to verify that the house will fit on that lot and meet the setback requirements in the local zoning code (see chapter 11). The **setback requirements** specify the distance (in feet) that the house must be set back from the road and both the side and rear lot lines of the property (see Figure 10-4). These setbacks are called the front yard setback, the side yard setback, and the rear yard setback. The municipality wants every neighborhood to look as if it was designed properly and would prefer that all the homes line up with each other as you look down the street. Depending on the size of the lot, you will have to build the house within the boundaries of the setback. Occasionally this will restrict the actual design and size of the home, as when yours is a narrow lot that is 100 feet wide at the road frontage. If the side yard setbacks are 20 feet on each side, then you have 60 feet in width to play with. If the house is

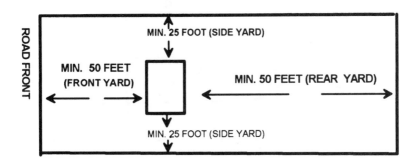

Figure 10-4. Yard setbacks.

to be 42 feet wide with an attached garage that is 20 feet wide for a total of 62 feet in width, you are 2 feet over the required setback and may have to make the house 2 feet smaller to fit the requirement. If your lot is located within a Planned Unit Development (PUD) or a master planned community, most popular in the western states, you may find that the setback requirements are very small or not there at all. This is known as a **0-lot line setback.** The developer wants to keep his development costs down, provide as much open space as possible, and provide an affordable sales price. Under this cluster concept, the homes are built on lots that are much smaller than the zoning requires. The side yard setbacks are usually the 0-lot where the house is built directly on the lot lines with a small area allowed in the front and rear of the house.

Figure 10-5 is a survey and topo of one of my lots in a small subdivision. The horizontal lines indicate the lot's elevation, which is measured at 5 foot intervals. The numbers on the left side of this topo indicate that the lot actually drops about 15 feet in elevation from front to back. The W represents the proposed well location, which must be a minimum of 100 feet from the edge of the proposed septic system location (S). If the well loca-

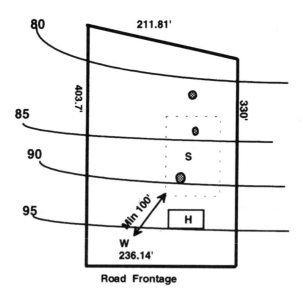

Figure 10-5. Topo lines.

tion were lower in elevation than the septic system, the separation would have to be at least 200 feet. The H marks the proposed house location. Because the soil on this lot has a heavy mixture of clay, the septic system will be of the fill-section variety. The small shaded circles are the three spots where the soil tests were performed. The overall lot size is 1.859 acres, or just about 81,000 square feet. You can also see that the lot drops down about 5 feet from the house to the septic system, which would ordinarily allow for good gravity feed into the septic system from the house. However, this system will require at least four feet of gravel fill, which will raise the top of the system to only 1 foot below the house. You can see that the septic area is much larger than the house area. Fill sections require a lot of space to allow for absorption and evaporation.

In this circumstance I would have to build the house a little higher to ensure enough gravity feed to the septic. Because the lot drains from the higher ground in the front to the lower area in the rear, I have to take the surrounding area into account, especially the land across the road, which I know is higher than my lot. To accommodate water draining from the road and from the land across the road, I will have to contour the land in the front of the house to create a small **swale** (ditch) that will allow water to drain away from the house and down one or both sides of the lot. Figure 10-6 illustrates this drainage strategy. An **after topo**

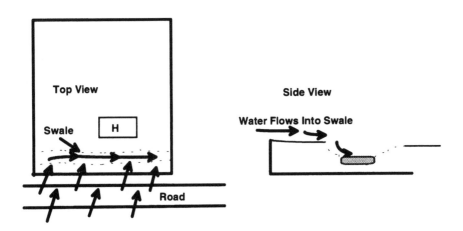

Figure 10-6. Top and side views of swale.

will need to be drawn up to document these changes to the lot's original contour; the original topo will then be called the **before topo.** Occasionally you will see the before and after topos on the same **plot plan,** which is a survey that has been fully engineered to show all the work required to make the lot usable.

To estimate the lot's actual percentage of grade, you estimate the amount of drop in elevation from the highest point to the lowest point and divide that number by the depth of the lot. Because most lots are not perfectly rectangular, it's OK to use an estimate just to get an idea of the elevations without going through complicated calculations. For this lot I estimate the drop to be about 15 feet from front to back. Fifteen feet divided by the depth of 330 feet equals 0.045, which means that the lot has about a 4.5 percent grade from front to back. Thus, this lot is fairly level with no steep grades, and I should be able to control the drainage without too much trouble. You can use this formula no matter how far apart the measurements are and visualize the lot without actually visiting the property. You can see how each property tells a story and how that story unfolds as you do your research.

Now you have an idea of how to measure the square footage of the property and calculate its elevations. You can see why a builder might need to build a foundation a little higher than it would be otherwise. You can inspect the lot with an eye toward existing or future problems. You can also check the building lot yourself before you involve the builder and gain some insight into the builder's or broker's statements regarding the lot.

11

WHAT IS ZONING?

Most municipalities today have incorporated as villages, towns, counties, or cities. When a municipality incorporates, it must file a charter, similar to that of a condo or co-op corporation, that specifies how it will conduct its business—how taxes will be collected, how trash will be removed, and so on. This chapter focuses on how a town may incorporate to avoid redundancy. Although municipalities may form their governments in different ways, they all operate basically the same way.

Usually a volunteer council of residents is formed to oversee the running of the town and elect a leader, such as a mayor or chief council member. However it is done, the leaders take the responsibility for the future growth of the town, which includes determining how various areas of the town can best serve the community. Sometimes professional planners are hired to advise the town on how to lay out future roads, where to build schools, where the best locations for industry are (usually near a railroad siding or on a river), where the best locations for commercial use are (usually along the busiest highways), and where and how to allow for the growth of residential development.

The council forms a **master plan** that divides the town into zones based on their highest and best use. If an area has access to central water and sewer services, you should find that the zoning code will allow a higher concentration of homes because soil conditions for wells and septic systems are not an issue. In areas without access to such services, the zoning codes will allow for larger building lots to accommodate on-site septic systems, soil conditions permitting. Sometimes, even though the land may be zoned for one-acre lots, the soil conditions will be such that the lots will have to be larger.

Based on the master plan, the town will publish a **zoning ordinance** that is adopted into town law. The law will regulate anything from lot size; lot configuration; driveway access; and front, side, and rear yard setback requirements to the maximum height a home can be built.

Most towns use even numbers to specify the lot sizes in a given area. Figure 11-1 is a portion of an actual zoning map; on it are several zoning designations, such as R-80 for 80,000-square-foot lots and R-40 for 40,000-square-foot lots. You can also see the darker boundaries of those zones and the areas that lie within those zones, including streets and roads.

When you've found a house that interests you, go to the local town or county offices and ask to see a copy of the zoning ordinance. Find the street or road where your target home is located, note the zoning classification for that area, look up the applicable zoning restrictions, and you will see how the zoning restrictions affect that particular lot—in other words, what you can and cannot do with that lot.

In Figure 11-1 you can also see sections zoned for commercial use such as C-1 and C-2. Other areas are labeled TC for Town Center Zoning; the town wants to preserve the country flavor of the central business district with zoning and building codes that are more restrictive.

HOW DOES ZONING WORK?

In one town near my home, all property that lies within an R-40 zone must be at least 40,000 square feet in area for a home to be built on it. The other designations for residential property are R-20 (a minimum of 20,000 square feet), R-15 (15,000 square feet), R-10 (10,000 square feet), and R-7.5 (7,500 square feet). These examples are simple and easy to remember, but unfortunately, al-

Figure 11-1. Zoning map.

most every municipality has its zoning drawn up by someone with different ideas, and each zoning ordinance contains designations that, although they accomplish the same control, may have different interpretations altogether.

You will find that a certain town may have one set of rules and a village within that town may have another. It's really fun when you own land that lies within two separate municipalities. For the purposes of this book, we will stay away from such complex zoning problems; when you have a better understanding of how zoning ordinances work, feel free to explore.

It is important to know the zoning laws that affect your target house, especially if you are buying a vacant lot for the purpose of constructing a new home or plan to make alterations to an existing house in the future. As I mentioned in the previous chapter, each zone has a specific requirement for setback distances, and they will affect the size and possibly the design of the home you wish to build.

In Figure 11-2 (not to scale), the lot is 100 feet wide and 125 feet deep, which means it is 12,500 square feet in area. Assuming the lot meets the square-footage requirement, you have to ascertain the setback requirements. According to the zoning, the front yard setback is a minimum of 50 feet from the edge of the road. The rear yard setback is a minimum of 40 feet from the back property line, and the side yard setbacks are 25 feet each. You can build your house anywhere outside the setback areas, so on this lot you can build a house up to 50 feet wide and 35 feet deep without violating the setback requirements for that zone. Let's walk through these calculations together. One hundred feet wide minus two 25-foot side yard requirements leaves 50 feet to build the house. Add the front yard and rear yard setbacks together to arrive at a total of 90 feet. Subtract that from the lot depth of 125 feet, and you see that you can build the house as deep as 35 feet if you want to. Multiply 35 by 50 and you get 1,750, which means that each floor can be as large as 1,750 square feet in area. You can make the house smaller or build the house in any configuration you want as long as you do not extend the house into any of the setback areas. Note that all the setback distances are

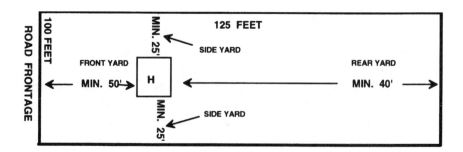

Figure 11-2.   Zoning Setbacks.

defined in terms of minimums. You can set the house back more than that specified distance but not less.

If you are buying an existing home, the zoning will affect how you use the property and sometimes prohibit further construction. If a proposed addition, such as a garage or a porch, extends beyond the setback requirements, you will not be allowed to build it. If you are looking at an existing home with plans to add space to it in the future, make sure that your plans will not violate the zoning ordinance's setback requirements.

Along with regulations for a myriad of items, even the size and color of for-sale signs, the zoning ordinance will set forth the **principal permitted uses** and **accessory uses** that are permitted in that zone. Table 11.1 is a limited version of how a typical zoning schedule will appear. The column farthest to the left designates the zone as R-40 or R-20 and so on. Moving to the right, you see the column that sets forth the permitted principal uses in that zone, followed by the column that designates the allowed accessory uses. The principal use is normally the highest and best use for the property. The accessory uses are more open ended, because that zone will encompass an entire district of a town. Check the principal and accessory uses allowed in the zone where your target home is located. If the zoning laws allow in-home commercial use or a conversion to multifamily use, the property has more value than others whose zoning does not allow multiple uses.

The next column designates the minimum lot size allowed in the zones, and the following columns set forth the front, rear, and side yard setback requirements. Make sure that your target home meets these requirements. If you are not sure, arrange a meeting with the zoning officer to explain your plans to ensure that the property will conform to the zoning laws.

If the existing home violates the setbacks, you (or preferably, the owner-taxpayer) could apply to the town for a **variance** from the zoning regulations regarding the setbacks. A variance is a request to vary from the existing ordinance, usually directed to a **zoning board of appeals** or a certain part of the town government that upholds the zoning laws.

To obtain a variance, you have to show the board that the home would be a welcome addition to the neighborhood; that to conform to the existing ordinance would create a hardship for

Table 11.1. Permitted Use Schedule

DIST.	PERMITTED USES	ACCESSORY USES	LOT SIZE (FT.)	LOT WIDTH (FT.)	LOT DEPTH (FT.)	FRONT YARD (FT.)	REAR YARD (FT.)	ONE SIDE (FT.)	BOTH SIDES (FT.)	MIN. FLOOR AREA (FT.)	MAX. LOT COVERAGE (%)	BLDG HEIGHT (FT.)
R-40	Residential	Churches	40,000	150	150	50	40	25	50	1,000	25	35
R-20	Residential	Town Buildings	20,000	100	125	40	40	15	30	900	25	35
R-10	Residential	Veg. stand	10,000	75	100	35	40	12	24	800	20	30
C-1	Commercial	Bowling	55,000	150	200	75	40	35	70	2,000	35	30

you or the lot owner, because homes in the area do not sell owing to their limited size; that the existing home was built prior to the zoning ordinance; or that the previous zoning change made the lot unmarketable. You will have to notify the surrounding property owners of your request and gain their approval. The board has the power to grant the approval no matter what the neighbors say, especially if other lots in the area have been granted similar approvals and a precedent has been set.

If most of the homes in the area are small and conform to the setbacks, you probably will not be granted a variance. However, if yours is a preexisting lot, that is, a lot whose boundaries were established before zoning existed or if the zoning changed after the lot was subdivided, the board may grant a variance because the original zoning would have allowed the larger home. In other words, the lot may be **grandfathered,** which means that because it existed before the currently applicable zoning laws were enacted, the town may agree to follow the previous zoning codes. If no zoning was in place, the town will probably agree to allow construction on the lot if the new construction or alteration will conform to the type or style of the existing homes in the general area.

Usually, the existing (taxpaying) owner of the lot is the one who should approach the zoning board of appeals because he has more right to ask for a variance than a potential buyer. However, you may be able to approach it as **contract vendee** or **owner-in-contract,** which means that you are the prospective buyer and potential future owner of the property. You would provide the board with a copy of the signed contract of sale as proof that you have an interest in the parcel and make your requests on that basis. In most cases, the present owner will have more influence over the board than a prospective buyer, but I've been before many zoning boards as a prospective buyer and achieved my goals.

HOW DOES ZONING AFFECT ME?

If you are buying an existing home, you must find out if any additions were made to the home **after** it was originally constructed. If additions were made, they should have been approved by the town building department or planning board, inspected throughout the construction process, and placed on a new, certified survey; as well, a new certificate of occupancy (c-of-o) should have been issued for the structure.

If none of this was done, the addition may be in violation of the town building codes and possibly the town zoning ordinance. It is possible the addition was built within the setback area required by the town, which would violate zoning law. The town could make you or the present owner tear it down. I have witnessed many prospective buyers fall in love with a particular home and spend time and money to process the purchase only to find near the end of the transaction that the home does not have a valid c-of-o or that an alteration was made without town approval and a violation exists. If this happens, you may lose your mortgage commitment owing to the time needed to investigate and correct the violation (if it is correctable), and everybody argues over who will pay for the correction. It is much safer to do your homework before making an offer or make the offer *subject to the lack of any violations against the property.*

Learning about the zoning ordinances and setback requirements also tells you what you can do to the property in the future. If you are buying a home that you plan to add to in the future, make sure that you have enough room to build the addition without violating the setback requirements before you buy the house.

The property may have been zoned to allow expansion when the original owner bought or built it, but zoning codes change over the years as the area grows, and new master plans are implemented. What was allowed before may not be allowed now, and you must make sure you can use the property for what you intended before you buy it.

If you have a problem, contact the building department and ask how it can be resolved. The town may grant you a variance to build the addition, but you're not going to buy the property unless you can do that. If you can persuade the present owner to wait long enough, make your purchase subject to the approval for the variance.

You want to check the zoning laws to see if the property can be used for other purposes besides single-family residence. You may be allowed multifamily use, which means you could convert the building into apartments in the future, or some limited commercial use may be allowed that would make the property more valuable if you wanted to start your own business or sell in the future to someone who has one.

Each zoning ordinance will be different, with a different set of required measurements and regulations pertaining to each zone. Zoning ordinances change all the time because of new master plans or simply changes adopted by the town board. Make sure that you find out about all of the changes that have occurred since the original ordinance was printed.

In any residential zone the property can be used for residential purposes. The permitted principal uses allow the owner to use the property for more than one purpose, such as an in-house office for a dentist or lawyer. You may need access to central water and sewer or satisfy any other requirement the town deems necessary to meet the goals of the area. For permitted principal uses you may have to apply for town board or town planning board approval, but if your property qualifies for the use in size and location, they shouldn't turn you down.

You may also find accessory uses permitted by planning board approval or by the issuance of a **special-use permit.** Accessory uses means more choices for uses for the property, but the town will require an in-depth study and the issuance of a permit for that use.

As an example, let's say that you own property in a residential zone, and you want to use it as a kennel. You have the required land area, and you wish to build additions to the existing building. If a kennel is a permitted principal use and you meet all the requirements to operate a kennel, the town must give you approval for the kennel unless there is an overwhelming negative reaction from the surrounding neighbors. If most of the neighbors object to the use for a kennel, the town may deny the use even though the zoning ordinance allows it. The town must always act for the good of the general public, and if it deems the use a hazard to the public welfare, it has the power to deny the allowed use.

If the community claims that they don't want a kennel, the town must act on behalf of the majority of the existing taxpayers and deny your request. If the town approves the kennel by issuing a special permit, it maintains control of the accessory use.

The permit must be renewed every year or so, and if a problem arises due to the accessory use, the town has the power to deny the permit in the future.

Find out what other uses are permitted for your zoning. If your property has more than one use, it adds to its value, and that price you thought was too high might just be a bargain.

12

WHAT IS TITLE?

Throughout this book, I have highlighted certain words by using **boldface** or *italic letters* to emphasize that those words have special meaning in the world of real estate. By your constantly repeating those words in the context of each chapter, you will become familiar with them and how they are applied to each circumstance.

In this and following chapters, the terminology becomes more technical. I will continue to highlight certain words or phrases of which you should be aware and understand how they will affect your purchase. As always, I will strive to follow the KISS theory and keep it simple.

To understand the concept of title to real estate, as opposed to title to your car, you must understand not only the *form* of ownership but also the difference between what is and is not considered real estate.

As I mentioned in chapter 1, the term *real estate* is composed of the words *real,* meaning not imaginary or artificial, and *estate,* which is the degree, nature, and amount of one's lawful interest in a property. When you buy real estate, you are buying real property. **Real property,** or **realty,** consists of the land and anything built upon, growing from, or affixed to the soil except crops grown for profit. These are considered *fructus industriales,* or "fruit of industry." Cash crops are personal property and do not belong to the real estate. Your car is personal property, not real property. **Personal property** is also known as **chattel property** because it does not meet the criteria for real property. Chattel property can be bought and sold with a handshake. For the sale of real property to be legally binding, it must be done in writing with adherence to a complete set of laws and regulations.

There are basically two forms of real property: **corporeal,** which is tangible, such as land and buildings, and **incorporeal,** which includes whatever rights are annexed to or exercisable with the land. In the chapter on surveys and topos, I mentioned encroachment, which occurs when someone builds over their property line and encroaches on another's property. A legal form of encroachment is the **right-of-way** (see Figure 12-1). You may buy a piece of property that has no existing road frontage but has a legal access road through the seller's or someone else's land. That access or permission to access another's property is known as a right-of-way and is used quite often.

A right-of-way is considered incorporeal property in that you do not actually own the land but have the right to use it. If you are interested in a property that allows access by right-of-way for you or another person, obtain a copy of the right-of-way in the county records, read it, and make sure that you understand what

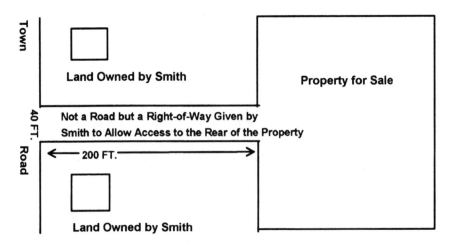

Figure 12-1. Example of a typical right-of-way situation.

rights are granted by it. Be sure that you understand who may use it, how it can be used, and for how long the right-of-way remains with the property. The right-of-way should show up on the certified survey; in fact, it should have its own survey to locate its exact boundaries, which should include a metes and bounds description to dispel any doubt as to the location of the right-of-way.

In the situation illustrated in Figure 12-1, Smith still retains ownership (in title) to the right-of-way but allows you to use that portion of his land to access your land. This is also known as an **easement by necessity** and usually cannot be denied to a land-locked parcel. Right-of-way access is fine as long as the right-of-way remains as a permanent deed restriction and continues to run with both Smith's deed and your deed. Legal documents can be written in almost any format for almost any reason to benefit anyone as long as they do not break the law. It is important to understand what may or may not affect your ownership and enjoyment of your property and what your rights are if that enjoyment is interrupted.

Another form of incorporeal property is the **easement,** which is a liberty, privilege, or advantage that one proprietor has in the lands of another without profit. A good example of an easement is a drainage pipe, water line, or sewer line extending through your property that was installed by the original developer and dedicated or assigned to the town when the project was completed. The easement will have been surveyed, and a metes and bounds description will have been drawn up similar to a deed; however, even though you still own the land on which the easement exists, the owner of the easement has certain rights to your land. An easement is considered **appurtenant,** which means it runs with the land (carries forward on future deeds). If the easement was created for sewer, water drainage, or underground utilities, the owner of the easement may have the right to enter your land for the purposes of repair or replacement of those services. If you are interested in a property that has an easement on it, make sure that the easement shows up on the certified survey and is explained in the deed. Figure 12-2 shows examples of typical easements.

Obtain a copy of the easement in the county records, read it, and make sure that you understand what rights are granted by it.

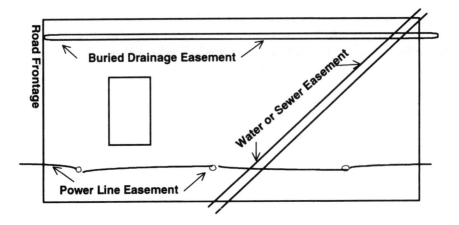

Figure 12-2. Examples of typical easements.

An easement or right-of-way may be considered an **encumbrance** if it has a dramatic effect on the free use of the property. If, for example, the only way to get to your property is to share a driveway with an adjoining neighbor and that joint use is not spelled out in a legal right-of-way agreement, then the property is **encumbered,** which creates a **cloud on title.** Most contracts of sale require the seller to transfer the title to the property free and clear of all liens and encumbrances. The title to your property is not clear owing to the adjoining owner's use of the driveway, which opens the possibility that the adjoining owner can claim future rights to continue the use of the driveway, especially if it is the main entrance into her property and she has used it for many years.

WHAT DOES *TITLE* MEAN?

The word *estate* refers to the **quantity** of ownership, and your **title** is evidence of that ownership. Your estate is considered a **freehold estate,** a term carried forward from the English feudal system.

There are two categories of freehold estate: **estates of inheritance** and **estates of noninheritance.** An estate of inheritance allows the right of ownership and the right to pass the estate on to your heirs. An estate of noninheritance allows certain rights that may only continue for a specified time.

Under the estate of inheritance, the highest type of ownership is called **fee-simple ownership.** Under the English feudal system, a king might grant a fee (a license) to his tenants to be held for their lifetimes with the right to pass the fee on to their heirs and assigns forever.

The fee-simple estate, or **fee-simple absolute,** involves three basic rights: the **exclusive right of possession,** which grants the owner complete control of the property; the **right of quiet enjoyment,** which allows the owner to utilize the property however he or she wants consistent with local laws; and the **right of disposition,** which allows the owner to sell, lease, or will his or her property to another. There are other forms of fee simple, but I promised to keep it simple, and fee-simple absolute is the form of ownership you should be interested in.

However, you should be aware of certain restrictions that may be placed on your ownership, such as **air rights.** Air rights are rights retained by the former owner or sold to others for the use of space above the ground, and they are primarily used in large cities where land has extreme value, such as in New York City, where Madison Square Garden was built over the Penn Central Railroad station. Water rights are another potential restriction, especially in areas of the Southwest where limited rainfall makes water very valuable. Other areas of restrictions may be for scenic rights in areas of natural beauty or for mineral rights, as in Pennsylvania, which maintains its rights to the state's abundant sources of coal.

HOW DOES TITLE WORK?

Real estate ownership is the act of owning, and the estate is what is owned. You may own real estate by **single ownership, multiple ownership,** or **joint ownership,** which is ownership by two or more persons and is also known as **tenancy in common** or **joint tenancy.**

Tenancy in common permits the ownership of unequal shares. Ownership may be created at different times, and the property may be proportioned according to each owner's interests. Tenancy in common may be used in a limited partnership situation or for the sale of a cooperative apartment.

Joint tenancy provides for a unity of interest, such as when a husband and wife own a home together. Ownership occurs at the same time; all parties possess the property together, and there is only one title listing of owners. In most states ownership by husband and wife constitutes **tenancy by the entireties,** which treats the husband and wife as one person. If one or the other spouse dies, the surviving spouse assumes full ownership by the **right of survivorship,** a feature not shared by tenancy in common.

HOW DO I OBTAIN TITLE?

When you want to purchase a home, you make a purchase offer and negotiate the purchase. Then you or the broker order a contract of sale to be drawn up, usually by the seller's attorney or the real estate agency (see chapter 14 for more information about purchase offers). The seller is required to transfer a **clear and marketable title free from all liens and encumbrances** to you. Your attorney or the escrow company will hire a **title abstract company** to search the **chain of title** to determine if there are any liens, encumbrances, judgments, or potential claims to the property by someone else.

The abstract company is normally owned by an attorney who has an affiliation with a **title insurance company.** The title insurance company will insure your title after the title attorney has researched the chain of title to determine if the title is clear and marketable. Sometimes a situation evolves in which your attorney has an interest in a title company and uses his own company to handle the title work. I feel that this situation creates a conflict of interest for the attorney. He is hired to protect you in all aspects of the purchase, and for that he will be paid his fee. I'm not comfortable with an attorney's involvement in any other aspect of the transaction.

Your purchase may be handled by an **escrow company.** The escrow company acts as a warehouse; it collects all of the documents, coordinates all activities, and brings the transaction to closing without the need for extensive use of the "legal Eagles."

The chain of title can be and often is traced back to the original creation of the property from land grants from the king of

England, the Louisiana Purchase from France, or the war with Mexico, listing all of the former owners of the property up to the present day. Most title companies do not need to travel that far back. Properties in this country have been bought and sold many times over the generations, and in this century, the title has been updated many times through the years. The title researcher might only go back to the sale to the previous owner or may go a little further, but most don't find an extensive search necessary unless there has been a question on a previous title search.

The **title report,** or **abstract,** will show any easement or encumbrances and any liens against the property such as mortgages or unpaid taxes. If the seller had financial or legal problems before the sale and someone filed judgments against her, it will show up in the title report.

The title attorney will also research the boundaries of your survey and compare them with the metes and bounds description on your deed to make sure that they match and the survey and lot description can close.

If the report is clean, you will buy title insurance from the title company. Title insurance is not mandatory if you are paying cash, but if you are financing the purchase, the lender will make title insurance mandatory. When you have title insurance, the title company guarantees your title. If someone comes up some day in the future with a claim to your property and the title company did not uncover that claim in its search, then the title company will be responsible for satisfying the claim if it is proven to be true.

Here's an example. One hundred years ago Mr. Smith owned a parcel of land, and he left the land to his nephew in his will. When Mr. Smith died, the nephew was not to be found, and his sister or wife sold the land. You now own all or a portion of that land, and suddenly a grandson of the nephew shows up, demanding that you leave his property. If the title insurance company did not uncover that break in the chain of title, it must satisfy the claim.

A chain of title is exactly what it sounds like. Each link in the chain represents a transfer of ownership. If one of the title transfers was not properly documented or recorded, there is a break in the chain. The title abstract company must research the chain to see if there has been a break, and if one is found, it will be reported in the title report.

I'll admit that this doesn't happen often, but it does happen. It's better to be safe than sorry, and the bank makes it a requirement anyway.

I have had the pleasure of having to research the chain of title on several properties and have met with success. If you have the time, I will tell you of one instance in particular. There was a problem with the title for a ten-acre parcel that I wanted to buy to subdivide it into five or more smaller building lots. The property had access to city water and sewer services, and after checking the zoning, soil conditions, and topography, I decided to buy the property.

The property's owner was an elderly man whom I will call Mr. Smith. He had inherited the land in the 1950s when his father died. However, when the title search was done, a break in the chain of title showed up owing to a confusing property description in the deed from the former owner to his father. After researching the deeds, I found that the property was part of an old subdivision dating back to the 1920s. The chain of title was OK up to the point where Mr. Smith's father bought the land. Apparently a valid deed had not been filed with the county. The printed portion of the only deed on file identified the property as parcel A and included a tax map designation, which we'll discuss in just a bit. The handwritten metes and bounds description, however, did not match up with the printed description, which did not contain a parcel A.

Because the actual (handwritten) deed description did not match any previous descriptions, the deed was not valid, and there was a break in the title chain. The title company would not insure the title unless there was a clear chain of title. I had been in the business for a good many years by this time, and I was intrigued by the challenge of uncovering the history of this title. I had to turn into a detective and try to track down the former owner or any of his relatives who might be in the area; I had to find someone or something that could verify that Mr. Smith's father bought the land. I started with the local telephone books and called anyone with the same name or even a similar name without success (it wasn't really Smith, thank God). His family had either died or moved from the area many years ago. Next, I tried to find the former owner's attorney, who had also died long ago. I questioned Mr. Smith and asked if he could remember his father's attorney's name; Mr. Smith did, but he had died long ago as well.

It was obvious to me that Mr. Smith owned the property and that his father had owned the property for many years. He remembered milking cows on the land when he was a boy. He had paid the taxes for over 40 years since his father's death, and no one else had come forward to claim the property in all of that time. I became determined to see this through.

My next step was to contact all the attorneys in the area to see if any of them knew about Mr. Smith's property, and there I hit pay dirt. A prominent local law firm had assumed the practice of the senior Smith's attorney. I asked where records relating to this property might be kept. I was informed that all the old records of the firm were kept in a local storage office, with a clerk on duty. Totally intrigued by this time with the history of the property and the story that was unfolding, I was elated to learn that the long lost original deed might just be left in an old file somewhere. I called the number given to me for the storage office and spoke to a soft-spoken woman whom I shall call Mrs. McCloud. I arranged to visit the office the next afternoon and found that it was located in an old building, in an older section of town, but I could see that at one time in the past the area had been very prosperous. I assumed that this was the original office of the senior Mr. Smith's lawyer, which proved to be true.

When I entered the building, I noticed the hall was poorly lighted, the wallpaper was stained and torn in spots, and the floor was bare (well-worn) wood. The entrance door to the office was ornate wood on the bottom, and the balance was mottled glass, the kind that looks as if someone tapped it with the ball of a hammer when it was still warm. Upon entering the office, I felt that I had been transported back in time to the late 1800s or early 1900s. The furniture consisted of wooden desks with wooden chairs and lamps that had to be decades old. Files were piled everywhere. I spied an old rotating fan on a shelf. My grandmother had given my parents a fan just like it before I was born (1947). The file cabinets that lined one wall had been painted a dark green about 50 or more years ago.

I remembered old *Twilight Zone* episodes and actually wondered whether I should run when Mrs. McCloud stepped in from another room. She looked at me with her head slightly cocked to one side and one eyebrow raised, and I quickly realized why. She was an elderly yet handsome woman of some 70 years of age, dressed in a white blouse tightly buttoned to the neck. Her skirt was solid black and ended just above two black button-top shoes. I couldn't help staring, considering the surroundings, and I must have looked as if I had seen a ghost, which was not far from the truth.

Fortunately, she broke the spell by offering her hand with a smile and greeted me with calm authority. To my relief her hand was warm; I immediately relaxed and launched into a full explanation of the problem with the deed while wondering if ghosts have warm hands. She invited me into her inner office where I was exulted to find an air conditioner in the window and a modern telephone and typewriter on her desk. With all doubts of reality cast aside, I was again both shocked and delighted to learn not only that Mrs. McCloud was the keeper of ancient records but also that when she was a young girl, she had been a secretary to the senior Mr. Smith's attorney. Even more amazing, she remembered the transaction when Mr. Smith purchased the property—what luck!

She agreed that the original deed could be somewhere in her office—or else Mr. Smith left it in a coat in an attic somewhere, and it had been long since lost. We began our search through the old records. After several hours of fruitless searching, Mrs. McCloud decided to open a very old filing cabinet, the kind made of heavy steel with a combination lock on it. After rummaging through the files, we found one with Mr. Smith's name on it.

I couldn't believe this was happening. It just could not be this easy; my anticipation level was rising through the roof. In the file we found the original handwritten (and somewhat yellowed with age) metes and bounds description from the former attorney that described the property in question, and then—Eureka! the original deed. Much to my dismay, however, the original deed also offered the legal description as parcel A, just like the one in the county records, without any other notes or further explanation as to why this letter was there.

I was back where I started from with the same unanswered question, although I did feel fortunate to have experienced the search, the excitement, the suspense, and most of all Mrs. McCloud. I shall always treasure the experience.

I wasn't finished just yet. I had to find out what the A represented because it was driving me nuts. I had not yet gone to the city assessor's office to check the old tax records. I went to the assessor's office, and after much smiling and groveling (on my part), the secretary descended into the basement and brought back the dusty tax rolls that dated back to just before the sale took place. When I looked up the **tax grid number** for that property, I finally found my answer.

At the time of the sale of the property to the senior Mr. Smith, the tax assessor's office used letters more than numbers as identification. The property in question was identified by the letter A together with a map number and block letter.

Apparently (and Mrs. McCloud agreed) when the attorney gave the original deed form to his secretary (unfortunately, not Mrs. McCloud) to fill in the details, she must have been late for lunch or something because instead of typing in the actual tax grid number or a reference to the attached metes and bounds description, she simply typed in the letter A, which was only a portion of the tax number. It was as simple as that.

The only way to clear the question on the deed was to petition the court for an action to **quiet title.** When no other means are available, you can ask a judge to settle the matter. We presented all the extensive research to the judge, who agreed that it was a matter of a simple typo. We advertised in several local papers for several weeks asking anyone who might claim an interest in the property to come forth and present evidence of a claim on a specified date; when no one showed up, the judge cleared the title to the junior Mr. Smith, who eventually sold the property to me.

Figure 12-3 shows the lot numbers from an actual tax map, which are map 6158, block or section 02, and lot number 230031. The legal description would read parcel 6158-02-230031. I presently own lot number 230031 and used the survey for this lot in my illustrations of surveys and setbacks in chapter 10. Although the tax map shows the lot size as 1.7 acres, the actual survey calculated the lot at 1.6 acres. The tax maps are used by the tax assessor to identify the lot for tax purposes only; the measurements of the house and lot are usually not accurate on a tax map. (NOTE: In certain western states, tax map numbers are not acceptable as a legal description; instead, the section block and

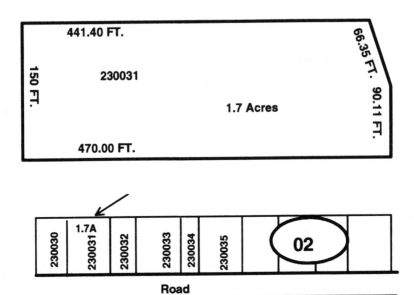

Map No# 6158

Figure 12-3.   Tax map description.

lot number of a subdivision are used—for example, Section 2, Block 5, Lot 231 of Cactus Estates.)

A tax map designation can be a legal description for a property when a metes and bounds description is not available, which is often the case for older properties in the East. The western states will accept only a metes and bounds description or a section, lot, and block number of a subdivision. A typical example may be 6158-02-125689. The first group of numbers, 6158, is the map number in the town or county assessor's office. The map is broken down into blocks to make it easier to locate a property, which accounts for the number 02. The last number, 125689, is the actual lot number within block 02 on map 6158. This identification can be any combination of letters or numbers depending on the town or county. The tax map number is also known as the **grid number** and can be used as a legal description with or without a metes and bounds description.

Whenever I look at a property, I go to the town or county tax assessor's office to locate the lot on the tax map. The tax maps are drawn on a smaller scale, which gives me an overall view of the surrounding lots in the area. On most tax maps you should find the dimensions of all of the lots in the area and all roads and streets as well as streams and rivers. Call it a detailed bird's-eye view that allows you to see how your target parcel relates to your neighbors' lots and where that parcel is located within the town.

13

WHAT IS A DEED?

In the early days of property transfer, the seller and buyer would walk on the land. The seller, now known as the **grantor,** would hand the buyer, the **grantee,** a clod of earth or a branch from a tree. An individual from the community who was able to write described the transaction on parchment paper. The seller signed the paper, and the writer (**scrivener**) applied his seal to the bargain.

The seller's (grantor's) signature is all that is required to this day. The seal, although still evident on many forms, is no longer required. All transfers relating to real property must be in writing; oral agreements are not considered legal transfers of title. **The deed is the proof of a legal transfer of title.** The deed is also considered a contract or bond because certain warranties are offered by the seller to the purchaser in the language of the deed. As an example, the seller warrants to the purchaser that the property is free from all liens and encumbrances except those stated in the deed.

There are three basic components to a deed in addition to the names of the buyer and seller (see Figure 13-1). The first is the description of the premises. The premises may be described by a lot number in a subdivision with reference to a **filed map number,** which is the number allocated to the map of the entire subdivision when the map was recorded in the county records. The

CONSULT YOUR LAWYER BEFORE SIGNING THIS INSTRUMENT. THIS INSTRUMENT SHOULD BE USED BY LAWYERS ONLY.

THIS INDENTURE, made the _____ day of 19_____, nineteen hundred and _____

BETWEEN

(the seller's name and address),

party of the first part, and

(the purchaser's name and address),

party of the second part,

WITNESSETH that the party of the first part, in consideration of Ten Dollars or other valuable consideration paid by the party of the second part, does hereby grant and release unto the party of the second part, their heirs or successors and assigns of the party of the second part forever, **ALL** that certain plot, piece, or parcel of land with the buildings and improvements thereon erected, situated, lying, and being in the (Town of Anywhere, State of Anywhere) and further described as beginning at a stake at the corner of a property owned by whomever and thence [so many] feet, [so many] degrees, and [so many] minutes south to a stake; thence [so many] feet, [so many] degrees, and [so many] minutes west to a stake; thence north [so many] feet, [so many] degrees, and [so many] minutes, to a stake; and thence east [so many] feet, [so many] degrees, and [so many] minutes to the point of the beginning, being further described as (insert tax grid number and street address),

TOGETHER with all right, title, and interest, if any, of the party of the first part in and to any street and roads abutting the above described premises to the center lines thereof; **TOGETHER** with the appurtenances and all the estate and rights of the party of the first part in and to said premises **TO HAVE AND TO HOLD** the premises herein granted unto the party of the second part, the heirs or successors and assigns of the party of the second part forever.

AND the party of the first part covenants that the party of the first part has not done or suffered anything whereby the said premises has been encumbered in any way whatever, except as aforesaid. **AND** the party of the first part, in compliance with Section 13 of the Lien Law, covenants that the party of the first part will receive this consideration

Figure 13-1. Example of a typical bargain and sale deed.

for this conveyance and will hold the right to receive this consideration as a trust fund to be applied first for the purpose of paying the
cost of the improvement and will apply the same first to the payment
of the cost of the improvement before using part of the total for any
other purpose. The word "party" shall be construed as if it read "parties" whenever the sense of this indenture so requires. IN **WITNESS
WHEREOF,** the party of the first part has duly executed this deed the
day and year first above written in presence of (insert witness's name).

Figure 13-1.   Continued.

description may read lot number 53, Wild Oaks subdivision;
map number 3300, filed in the county clerk's office on August 1,
1993. There may or may not be a metes and bounds description
(see chapter 10).

Another description may be the tax grid number, which identi-
fies the lot by map, block, and lot number (see the previous chapter). However, there may be a complete metes and bounds description that located the lot on the face of the earth, together with
the measurements of the lot. The metes and bounds description is
the best you can get, but sometimes one may not be available, and
you may use one or more of the other forms of description.

The second component is the **Habendum** clause, which means
"to have and to hold." The Habendum defines the quantity of the
property that is transferred by the grantor. The grantor transfers
all rights, title, and interest to the grantee. The third component
is the **Testimonium.** This section includes the warranty by the
grantor that the premises is free and clear, and "in witness
thereof," the grantor signs the deed in the presence of a notary
public.

The deed will be dated, usually at the top. The seller (grantor)
will be identified as the **party of the first part,** and the buyer
(grantee) will be identified as the **party of the second part.** The
next section may set forth an acknowledgment that a **consideration** has been paid, which could be $1 or $10, and that the seller
grants and releases the property to the buyer (this is known as
the **granting clause**), his heirs, successors, and assigns forever.
The next section is another description of the property, which
should include a **liber and page** number of any **covenants and**

restrictions of record. In the western states, these are known as **CC&Rs: Conditions, Covenants, and Restrictions.** Covenants or restrictions are any terms within the deed by which the new owner must abide, such as a square-footage restriction on the size of the home placed by the land developer. The liber and page number refers to the book (liber) that contains the existing and former deeds to the property and to the specific page in that book on which this information is to be found.

You can go to the county clerk's office, look up the seller's name in the book or file under grantees for when they bought the property, find the liber and page containing the deed, and see when they bought the property and from whom.

Here's a neat little trick. If your target state collects taxes on property transfer, there should be a stamp with a dollar figure in it on the deed. The taxes are charged on the basis of so many dollars per thousand of the purchase price at that time. Ask someone at the desk what that formula is, and you can find out how much the seller paid for the property. For example, let's say the tax stamp reads $100 and the formula is $1 per $1,000. The seller bought the property for $100,000. If you want to get really nosy, find the records under mortgagees. (Remember this from the chapter on mortgages?) Look up the seller's name and find the liber and page that shows his or her mortgage. Calculate the payments from the time they bought the property, and you know not only how much he or she paid for it but also how much is still owed on it. That information might come in handy when it's time to negotiate the price. Keep these tricks under your hat!

The next section will transfer all **appurtenances** to the grantee, which are any rights to streets, roads, alleyways, light, air, and existing rights-of-way and easements. The last section of the deed will be the **acknowledgment,** which contains the seller's signature and is witnessed, usually by an attorney or notary public. This also establishes the deed's authenticity and allows the deed to be recorded. The acknowledgment will also note the venue or county and state where the transaction took place.

In certain states, a separate acknowledgment must be taken by husband and wife to affirm that they are signing of their own free will. This separation is a carry over from the days when a husband might gamble away the homestead without the wife's knowledge.

WHAT TYPES OF DEEDS ARE THERE?

Warranty Deed

The **warranty deed** is a popular form of title transfer. The seller warrants that she is in fee-simple ownership, that she has the right to convey the property, and that there are no liens and encumbrances (covenants at the present time) against the property other than those made public. The seller personally guarantees the truthfulness of these statements and can be held accountable in a court of law if the grantee finds otherwise.

The seller further warrants quiet enjoyment of the property to the grantee, which means that in the event someone pops up with a prior claim against the property, the seller is obligated to satisfy the claim by working together with the title company. This type of deed is also known as a **full covenant and warranty deed.** Simply put, if any information provided by the seller to influence you to buy the property turns out to be untrue, you have legal recourse against the seller.

Deed of Trust (Trust Deed)

A **deed of trust** is used in the western states and requires a third party, in most cases a lender. The seller conveys the property; the buyer pays the down payment and offers a mortgage for the balance. The lender (or other third party) holds onto the deed until the mortgage has been paid in full and then surrenders the deed to the buyer.

Quit Claim Deed

The **quit claim** is a **dangerous** way to acquire title to a property. This type of deed means just what its label implies; the grantor simply quits and releases any interest or potential interest he or she may have in the property with no covenants or warranties at all. The key words are "remise, release, and quit claim."

A quit claim may be used during a dispute between property owners over a section of land. To solve the dispute, one owner quit-claims the land to another, fast and simple. Sometimes, when counties seize property for back taxes, they transfer title by quit claim deed at an auction. Because the county was not the former owner and did not have a warranty deed, they simply quit-claim the property.

The danger in using this instrument is that you have absolutely no title protection in the event of a dispute. It is difficult to obtain title insurance with a quit claim deed, and you may have to start an action to quiet title in court to obtain clear title. Also, there may be past debts filed as liens against the property from creditors that were not satisfied by the former owner. If you buy the property by quit claim, those past debts may become yours.

Bargain and Sale Deed

This form of deed establishes that consideration has been transferred, in some form, between buyer and seller. The consideration has to have a tangible value such as money or something equivalent. For the purposes of property transfer, consideration of at least $1 is sufficient. You can purchase property with a truckload of chickens if you can convince the seller to accept them. Although there are other forms of deed, these three are the most widely used. To receive the most protection in a deed, ask the seller to provide a **Bargain and Sale Deed with Covenant against Grantors' Acts,** which is considered a **Full Covenant and Warranty Deed.** The bargain and sale deed with covenants combines the protection of a warranty deed and establishes that consideration was paid to obtain the warranty used in the bargain and sale deed. In other words, you paid for the protection of the warranties given by the seller, and you are entitled to them.

I think we have covered everything you should know to follow through with the purchase. Let's do just that in the next chapter on negotiating, purchase offers, and contracts.

═══ **14** ═══

HOW DO I BUY IT?

Buying a home is one of the most important decisions you will make in your entire life. In most cases, your decision will dramatically affect your financial future for many years as well as your family's quality of life. If you are a first-time home buyer, you will probably experience an abundance of emotions, from excitement to outright fear, regarding the final decision. As I explained in chapter 1, millions of people are buying homes every year, and with the benefit of this book, your decision to buy is an educated one.

To reach this point, you have:

- Determined which buyer group you belong to, first-time or move-up
- Verified the size and style of the home you need
- Qualified yourself for the amount and type of mortgage you need
- Pinpointed the geographic area that meets your needs
- Qualified the sales agent
- Qualified the location of your new neighborhood
- Inspected various homes regarding their condition

194

- Established an idea of property values in your target area
- Learned about water tables, radon, radiation, wells, and septic systems
- Learned about surveys and topography
- Learned about zoning and how it affects your purchase
- Learned about what title is and the types of deeds involved in estate

Having accomplished all of this, you should have a good idea of the condition and market value of the property. The goal now is to buy the property at the best price and terms that you can get.

When the time comes to begin the purchase process, emotions and doubts sometimes begin to creep into the picture and cloud a buyer's judgment. Think about it. If you have followed the process set forth in this book and found a home that meets your needs and you have done your homework regarding size, age, condition, market value, lot condition, and more, then you have accomplished the hardest part of the task. You should feel very confident at this point in making the move to purchase. There are just a few more steps to take to achieve success and assume ownership.

If you feel comfortable that the property falls within your price range and the asking price is within market value, you should be able to begin the negotiating process without feeling doubtful about this next step. I have been in this business for more than 20 years, and with very few exceptions, there is room in every deal for negotiation.

You have to think about your own situation before you structure the offer. If you are transferring into the area to begin a new job and your family needs to get settled quickly, you don't want to lose the house or delay the purchase any longer than is necessary. At the same time, you do not want to pay more than is necessary.

When a sales agent takes a listing for a house, the owner usually has two numbers in mind. The first number is how much he would like to receive from the sale, and the second number is what he would be willing to accept from the sale. Depending on the market conditions in the area, the first number is most likely based on emotion and will be too high.

The owner has lived in the house for a while and may have added living space or achieved a certain personal style of decoration. He may have made improvements along the way such as adding new ceramic tile or kitchen cabinets or a swimming pool or something that makes the property his personal home, and he is proud of it. His children may have been born and raised there, and there are years of memories associated with the house—although in today's rotating society this is becoming less and less of a factor.

The sales agent understands the owner's (seller's) feelings and needs and may accept the listing for the house even if the initial price is too high for the current market. The agent should have explained the current market to the seller and advised him that if the house doesn't sell within 30, 60, or 90 days, he should be willing to reduce the price to current market values if he is to sell the house within the desired time frame.

Unless the area is booming and homes are selling at a record pace, a certain amount of time will pass before the seller feels willing to negotiate. After 30 days the seller starts to become a little anxious but still feels the house is worth it. After 60 days he begins to think the sale is not going to be as easy as he first thought. After 90 days he starts to wonder how long it's going to take, and after 120 days he is usually anxious to get it over with.

Ask the sales agent how long the house has been on the market; how many offers have been made, if any; what the original asking price was; and if there have been price reductions and how much they were. You need to find out where the seller stands before you can begin to ask him to give something up. Remember that the second number is the bottom-line number. If the house has been on the market for a long time and the seller has already reduced the price to current market value or lower, don't expect him to go much lower than that unless his situation is desperate.

The sales agent should have information regarding the final sale prices for similar homes, but the agent has a fiduciary responsibility to the seller unless you are working with a buyer's agent, and even then she may be restricted from providing you with that information.

There is no set rule of thumb for making an offer, but in my experience, there should be a cushion of approximately 15 percent in the price to be used as negotiating tender. Remember, the seller has to pay the broker's fee and his own set of closing costs and probably the balance of a first mortgage before he can put any money in his pocket. The seller also has to pay for the costs of moving and the costs of buying or renting a new home somewhere else, and these expenses will be very much on his mind.

I have always found that if I can achieve most of what I need and the other person can achieve most of what he or she needs, there is a deal to be made.

Make the offer for less than what is asked; try for 15 percent or even 20 percent less than the asking price. If the area is economically depressed and homes are not selling quickly, you might try an offer of 25 percent less. You know in your mind that the asking price you were presented with falls within the current market value; if you can buy it for less, that's great. If you must buy it at the current market value, you are still not paying too much. Any price at or less than market value should be acceptable.

If you are a first-time buyer, your level of anticipation will probably be rising. Relax, sit back, and think about it. This is an important decision, and you need a clear head. **Always, always,** and again, **always,** keep in the back of your mind that no matter how hard you try or how far you bend and how much in love with the property you may be, it may not work out. It doesn't hurt to have one or more homes you may have seen and liked as a backup just in case your first choice doesn't work out. However you structure the offer, do not allow your emotions to overcome your common sense and overpay; in most cases, it is a mistake you will regret.

One way to absolve myself when a deal does not come together no matter how much work I put into it or how hard I try is to tell myself that deals are made in heaven. If it is meant to be, it will be; if not, I'll go on to the next deal. Keep it simple!

You will probably use an attorney for legal advice when you reach this stage, and it's important to know a little about attorneys. In some areas in the western part of the country, home sales may be handled by an escrow company. Contracts may be drawn by the real estate broker, but coming as I do from an area ruled by lawyers, I would be hesitant not to involve an attorney with such a large and complicated purchase.

This is the time to set the stage for all future negotiations. There is an *unwritten awareness* in this business when negotiating to the effect that "he who cares the least wins." If you become all excited about the house and tell the sales agent that you just have to have it, the sales agent, obligated to the seller in most cases, will convey that information to her. The seller will become more confident, and it may cost you money.

Inform the sales agent that you like the house and want to make a purchase offer but make it known that if this deal does not work out, you will continue looking. Let the sales agent know that you are interested in several other homes in the paper that are advertised with other brokers. This places the sales agent on notice that he could lose a commission and it should affect the way he presents the offers to the seller. If the offer falls through, nobody gets paid.

HOW DO I QUALIFY AN ATTORNEY?

I may not make too many friends in the legal profession with this section of the book, but based on my experiences over the years dealing with many attorneys, I feel qualified to offer some criticism and praise where it is warranted.

I have learned that there are two basic types of attorneys: **deal makers** and **deal breakers.** A deal maker knows the business, is comfortable in her profession, has experience, and works for the best interests of her client. A deal maker will advise her client of the pros and cons throughout the entire process, explain each phase of the process, and make sure her client understands each agreement and legal form he is expected to sign. A deal maker will try to resolve any differences or problems that may arise in a professional and timely way, with the thought in mind that her client wants to buy this house and that goal must be reached. A deal breaker, on the other hand, is only interested in controlling the entire deal (because he is smarter than anyone else, including his client), and the last course in which he received high marks in law school was titled "I am God 101." A deal breaker is always too busy to meet with his clients, and any meetings must be on the attorney's schedule at a place and time dictated by the attorney. The deal breaker doesn't return phone calls from his client, no matter how many calls are received, until the client becomes overly frustrated and demonstrates to the attorney's secretary (who has been brainwashed to take all of the flak) that the client needs the attorney to save the day. The deal breaker does not fully explain the process of the transaction, and neither does he take the time to explain the legal significance of each document that his client is expected to sign—because he is smarter than his client, why waste the time? The deal breaker becomes involved in the negotiations with the seller's attorney regarding the terms and conditions of the sale.

Do not let your attorney negotiate the purchase! If your attorney is a deal breaker and becomes involved, she will only become entangled in a contest with the seller's attorney to see who is smarter, and your concerns will not matter. I mentioned that I will not make many friends with this section, but I have experienced both types of attorneys many times over the years right up to this very day.

The purchase of the home is your purchase. You did all the work, and you are taking all the risk. You hired your attorney to advise you of the pros and cons and to work with the other parties involved to make the purchase happen, not to become involved in the negotiations. The attorney will never see the house, knows neither where it is nor what it is worth, and is not qualified to change the deal once one has been approved unless there is a situation regarding the law where advice is needed.

The deal breaker will come up with several totally unnecessary and unreasonable conditions to the transaction that will anger everyone involved and produce enough frustration to force either the buyer or seller to throw in the towel when the deal could have been made. At the same time he will extol his experience and spout about protecting you. Believe me, when the deal falls, you will receive a bill for legal services.

Another type of deal breaker is the one who, because she is soooo busy, does not respond to phone calls from anyone. She also does not follow up on the progress of the sale and always needs something faxed to her. She does not produce the proper documentation when it is needed and will usually notify you that something must be signed about 15 minutes before it must be submitted.

There is absolutely nothing wrong with asking the attorney to provide you with several references from past or current clients.

You are hiring the attorney to perform a service. Check him out the same way you check out a mechanic or doctor.

You negotiate the price and terms of the sale. You advise your attorney that this is the price and these are the terms and let both attorneys earn their fees over the fine points of the legal language in the agreements. I don't mean to sound so cynical about lawyers. I have had the pleasure of dealing with many very fine attorneys, but some of them are more concerned with their egos then they are with their clients' interests. If you have an attorney in mind and he or she fits the profile of a deal breaker, then find someone else. Believe me, you will not regret it.

If you have an attorney that you or your family has worked with in the past but you are moving in from another state or county, consider finding a local attorney. I do not imply that because the attorney is not local, she can't do the job, but if the attorney has not established a working relationship in the area with other attorneys, brokers, or banks, he or she will be at a distinct disadvantage. She may not even know where your new town is on the map. Like a new kid on the block, the out-of-town attorney will have to be overly cautious because she is unfamiliar with the local ground rules. Although most house closings are basically the same, local customs vary from one area to another. A property transaction in lower Westchester County, New York, is a little different from a sale in Duchess County, New York, just 40 miles away. If your attorney is in the position of not knowing the area or local professional customs, she will tend to be overprotective and make the transaction cumbersome. The original contract of sale is drawn up by the seller's (usually local) attorney, who then sends it to your attorney. Your attorney makes major changes to the original agreement, adding pages and pages of protection, and the contest begins between the attorneys. If you can find local representation, the deal should progress much faster and easier. If your attorney has a tendency to make things complicated, then remind her to keep it simple. A good source for finding local attorneys is the sales agent. It is unethical for a sales agent to recommend a buyer to a particular attorney, but over time the agent will have experienced transactions with most of the local legal-eagles and can recommend several that can give you good representation. If you have obtained a list of previous buyers from the sales agent, give them a call, ask how they liked their attorney, and narrow it down to the best choice. As always, if you keep it simple and if you are courteous and provide your lawyer with what she needs on a timely basis, the deal should run smoothly.

WHAT IS A PURCHASE OFFER?

I'm sure by now that you have heard the terms **binder** or **purchase offer.** This is your first move to purchase the property, where the negotiations begin and where you become a serious buyer. You have done all of your investigations and are confident that you are ready and qualified to buy this property. The phrase most often used in the industry is that you are now **ready, willing, and able** to buy. When you are ready to make an offer, the sales agent will ask you to sign a purchase offer or binder form and pay a **good-faith deposit,** which may be anything from $100 to 1 percent of the total purchase. An example would be a purchase offer of $100,000 with a good-faith deposit of $1,000. Write **initial binder** or **good-faith deposit for purchase of** on the check, followed by a description of the property. Make the check out to the realty company **as trustee,** not the sales agent or individual broker. The check must clearly state that this payment is only for a binder, not a down payment. In certain areas of the country, it is customary to sign a formal contract of sale when you make the initial offer instead of a purchase offer or binder. Read the information in this chapter on what constitutes a formal contract. If you are required to sign a formal contract with your offer, you may be required to pay a deposit of as much as 10 percent of the purchase price. If you plan to use an attorney to represent you in the purchase, make the contract contingent upon your attorney's review and approval and make sure that your check is made out to an escrow or trustee account and not to an individual.

The binder form should contain the following:

- The amount of the deposit received by the broker and the date it was received
- The names and addresses of both buyer and seller
- The address of the property

- The offered price and terms and contingencies
- The projected dates for signing of formal contracts and closing
- A list of any personal property included in the sale
- Notes for any other agreements or conditions
- A **contingency clause (subject-to clause)** that this sale is contingent on the buyer obtaining the required financing and any other contingencies
- The names, phone numbers, and addresses of all parties involved

A typical purchase offer is shown in Figure 14-1.

The contingency clause is one of the most important clauses in this agreement and the formal contract. The purchase may be contingent on almost anything, from dyeing your shoes a different color to obtaining bluebirds to populate the property. However, in reality most contingency clauses relate to the necessity for the buyer to obtain a mortgage of a certain amount for a certain length of time at a certain interest rate to qualify for the purchase.

Sometimes the offer to purchase a new house is contingent on the buyer selling and closing title of his former residence. This is what I call your **out clause.** I always try to leave myself a way out of the deal if something comes up later that may be a problem.

For the purposes of a binder, you should include all of your contingencies. This notifies the seller of your needs and avoids the necessity of having attorneys involved in negotiating the fine points of the contract. Once the negotiations are complete and you have an accepted purchase offer, the seller's attorney will be notified to draw the **formal contracts of sale** (in some areas of the country, the real estate broker will draw the formal contracts).

There are **six** basic elements that make up a formal contract. Read the section in this chapter **before** you sign the binder or purchase offer.

If the purchase offer or contract includes certain contingencies required by the buyer and the buyer does not act upon those contingencies and later decides to back out of the deal, the seller may claim a default by the buyer on the agreement and make a claim to keep the initial deposit. An example would be if you in-

AYZ REAL ESTATE
PURCHASE OFFER AGREEMENT

Received as deposit $_____   Date _____

I(We) _____

offer to purchase property at _____

from _____ as Sellers

Terms of this offer as follows:

Sale price   _____

This deposit   _____

Due upon contract signing _____

Due at closing   _____

Contracts to be signed on or about _____

Closing to be on or about _____

Personal property included in sale _____

_____

_____

Other
agreements _____

_____

This agreement is conditioned upon the Purchaser obtaining
☐ Conventional ☐ FHA ☐ VA mortgage from a lending institution
for the amount of

$_____

Purchaser _____

Seller _____

Figure 14-1. A typical purchase offer.

cluded a contingency to obtain a certain amount of financing but
neglected to apply for the financing on time (you waited too
long). If you include a contingency in any agreement, it is your
responsibility to resolve that requirement on a timely basis.
When the purchase offer is signed by both buyer and seller, the
seller's house is effectively off the market. Backup binders may

be taken for other offers, but you are first in line and are responsible to the seller to follow through as quickly as possible.

Any agreement that can be interpreted as a legally binding contract is enforceable in a court of law if it meets certain criteria, even if it is labeled as a binder (again, refer to the section on contracts).

As an example, several years ago I negotiated a purchase for a 20-acre parcel of land that I intended to subdivide into 10 or more building lots. I signed a purchase offer; rendered a good-faith deposit check, which I simply labeled as a "deposit"; and made the purchase subject to all of the surveying, engineering, and tests required to receive approval.

The initial contingency was that I be allowed to test the soil and perform certain preliminary engineering before signing formal contracts to find out if the property could produce what I thought it could. Because it was a sizable parcel, even the preliminary work took several weeks and was rather expensive. Upon completion of the investigative work, I indicated to the broker that I was ready to proceed with formal contracts. He informed me that the owners had changed their minds and decided not to sell. We argued back and forth, but the owners refused to budge. I was not happy about the prospect of losing all the money and time I had put into the project and carefully reviewed the original binder agreement. The agreement (as written) provided for all the requirements of a formal contract. I indicated to the broker that I was willing to pursue the purchase in court if the sellers backed out. After careful review of the agreement, the seller's attorney agreed that the purchase offer was, in fact, a binding contract, and the purchase went through.

This may sound as if I was playing hard ball, and I was. In the investment end of this business, you have to be incredibly careful; after all, I had spent thousands of dollars I could not afford to lose. I found out later that once the owners found out (at my expense) that the property had potential, they decided to subdivide it themselves. There is justice in the world.

THE ART OF THE DEAL

You may or may not have to haggle over the price, but it is to be expected that you will make an **initial offer** that is lower than the asking price. When the sales agent accepted the listing, I'm sure she explained the procedure to the seller, and because the seller is already a home owner, he is familiar with it.

You can expect to receive a **counteroffer** from the seller for less than the asking price but more than your offer, and so the process goes back and forth until you get down to the seller's second number or bottom line and your financial ability to purchase.

I must note that prices for newly constructed homes are not normally negotiable. It is accepted in most areas that the price is fixed and the builder is offering the property at the best price possible. Who started this custom? The builders. Why? Because they don't want to negotiate the price. If an area is booming and new construction is moving well, chances are you won't be able to negotiate the price. If the area is not selling well, negotiating might save you some money. Most builders price their homes with a minimum markup and sell in volume. Don't expect a substantial decrease in price, but you might save something.

When the offer and counteroffer parade is almost finished— and it may take anywhere from several days to several weeks— emotions are usually running higher than when the process began. You have learned that the owner is flexible, and he has learned that you are flexible, and you are getting close to a deal. He is thinking of his new home, and you are already planning where the furniture will go and what color to paint the rooms. Slow down. Relax, think about it, and keep it simple. The price may be within a few thousand or even a few hundred dollars of both of your goals. Remember, you are the one who cares the least. When you are this close to a deal, you can do one of four things. You can accept the last counteroffer from the seller and go to contract; you can compromise with another counteroffer; you can be nice and offer to split the difference 50–50 with the seller; or you can play hard ball and say that you won't go any higher. Again, depending on everyone's circumstances, playing a little hard ball is not a bad thing as long as it's done in the right atmosphere. Also remember, a little honey gets better results than a little vinegar.

You can say "no way, if he wants more, the deal's off," or you can say, "I am at my limit; I can't afford to go higher." The first presentation is confrontational; the second is conciliatory. Which one would you respond favorably to? Try it—if it doesn't work, you can always offer to split the difference or raise the offer, or you could look for another house.

Remember, if homes in the area are selling quickly, you may not have the advantage of time to play the negotiating game. In such cases, as long as the purchase price is at or below market value, buy it.

When the deal is down to the wire—and I'm not going to make any friends among sales agents with this advice, but this is the real world—ask the broker to participate by accepting a few dollars less for her commission to put the deal to bed. This request should actually come from the seller because he is paying the commission, but it doesn't hurt to suggest it to the broker. Depending on the volume of business the office does (remember the law of supply and demand), it is not uncommon for a broker to lower her fee if the deal is very close and business is slow. The focus of everyone's concerns is to put the deal together, and everyone wins when that happens.

I've always felt it would save time if everyone simply stated their respective bottom lines up front. But that would take all of the fun out of it.

WHAT IS A CONTRACT?

I begin this section by stating that I am not an attorney and am not licensed to practice law in any state. Further, any explanations I offer are based on my own experiences, and any opinions I offer are simply that, my own opinions. Because I am not a licensed lawyer, I cannot offer you formal legal advice. With that said, I will now offer you my experienced opinions. For formal legal advice, I advise you to speak to a licensed attorney.

Contract forms will vary from state to state, and you can usually find them in any stationery store. Buy one and read it through to get an idea of what they look like.

There are six basic conditions that must be met for any agreement to be construed as a legally binding contract:

1. There must be an offer to buy, and the offer must be accepted.
2. There must be some form of consideration paid.
3. The agreement must be signed by competent parties.
4. The agreement must be free of fraud, misrepresentations, or mistakes and not signed under any undue influence.

5. The agreement must be legal and not in violation of state or federal statues.

6. The agreement must be in writing.

If any agreement meets these criteria, even if it is written on tree bark, it is enforceable in a court of law. When you are a party to a contract, you (the buyer) are now known as the **contract-vendee,** and the seller is known as the **contract-vendor.** Both of you are also now referred to as a **party** or **parties to an agreement.**

In certain areas of the country, formal contracts may be prepared by the real estate broker, and in others it is customary (and sometime required by law) for a licensed attorney to prepare contracts. Regardless of who prepares the formal contract of sale, it must meet those six criteria.

To meet the offer and acceptance rule, there must have been a **meeting of the minds** between buyer and seller. This occurs when the buyer and seller agree on the final price and terms of the sale and the agreement is formalized with a formal contract of sale. In most states, the real estate broker is not entitled to a commission unless buyer and seller achieve a meeting of the minds.

Although in most areas a formal contract is not enforceable unless consideration is paid, usually in money (unless you have a truckload of chickens), in some states a promise of payment may be enough to make the contract enforceable. The initial deposit and down payment is known as **earnest money,** which tells the seller that the buyer is earnest (serious) and capable of consummating the sale.

For the parties to be considered **competent,** they must be of an age that meets state law requirements. In most states that age is 21 years. It's hard to believe in this day and age, but certain states may require a female buyer, if married, to obtain her husband's signature on the contract, whether he is part of the purchase or not. The parties cannot be mentally incompetent (even though you might feel like it at this point); both parties must be in control of their mental faculties and capable of understanding the agreement.

The agreement cannot be riddled with mistakes or include any language that would be considered fraudulent. The agreement must not include anything or be signed by anyone under duress or a stressful situation. The language must be clear and concise and written in such a way that there should be no misconceptions by either party. This is called the **reality of consent.** The contract must be real.

The contract cannot violate local, state, or federal laws to be enforceable. It cannot interfere with local governmental regulations or be injurious to the general public. This is known as the **legality of the object.**

Finally, the agreement must be in writing. It can be written on almost anything as long as it meets these criteria and is legible. If you were to write the contract on tissue paper, it would be legal and binding.

Fortunately, many states now require what is known as a **plain language contract.** For the most part, they are written in plain English without all of the heretofores, theretofores, and hereinafter referred tos that attorneys are so fond of.

If you want to see an original contract, ask your attorney or broker what type of form is customarily used in the area. Then go to an office supply store, buy one, and read it through.

In the eastern sections of the country, it is customary for the seller's attorney to prepare the formal contract of sale and send it to the buyer's attorney. In the West it is customary for the real estate sales agent or brokers to prepare the contract of sale.

Because all of my experience was acquired in the Northeast, where attorneys hold control over most legal issues, and because attorneys are educated in all facets of the law pertaining to real estate, I am accustomed to buying and selling with an attorney available to advise me. This is probably the largest investment you will ever make, and the issue involves a host of legal ramifications, so I recommend that you hire an attorney to review the documents anyway.

If you obtain a copy of a printed contract, review it paragraph by paragraph to become familiar with the basic format a contract can take. No matter who prepares the contract, ask to review the document line by line if you need to verify your understanding of what you are expected to sign. **Be comfortable with it before you sign it.**

When you have reviewed the contract, made whatever changes to it that are appropriate, and signed it, then you are considered **bound by the agreement** if all the criteria for a legal binding contract have been met.

The contract will include the names and addresses of the buyer and seller, a legal description of the property to be sold, and a schedule for how the money is to be paid. Other paragraphs will describe any existing mortgages or liens against the property that have to be satisfied and what may happen in the event of a default by the parties.

In my experience, most buyers do not take the time to read the contract thoroughly to obtain a complete understanding of what they are signing. They take for granted that whoever prepares the contract knows what they are doing, and because this is done on a regular basis, as long as the buyer sees his requirements on the agreement, the balance of the agreement is so much legalese.

Read it anyway. Remember, the seller's attorney prepared the agreement to protect the seller, not you.

You will have certain contingencies entered into the agreement to protect you in the event that those conditions cannot be met. You will most likely need a mortgage to purchase the property. The size of the mortgage, the number of years needed to pay it off, and even the required interest rate can be entered into the agreement, which would make the agreement contingent on your obtaining the required mortgage. You may have negotiated with the seller to leave the appliances or lawn mower with the house, and that should be entered into the agreement as personal (**chattel**) property included in the sale. **Oral agreements** made to purchase personal property such as a refrigerator or lawn mower before the signing of a formal contract may not be legally valid. Certain states have laws known as **Parol Evidence Rules,** under which oral agreements are not considered enforceable unless they were made after the signing of a formal written agreement. Make sure that all of your agreements with the seller are in writing; there are no mistakes that way. If a contingency is entered into the agreement by either the buyer or seller and that contingency cannot be met, the agreement can be considered **null and void by either party.**

Make sure that the agreement reads so that if all or part of a certain contingency cannot be met, the agreement can be considered null and void, and all deposit money paid by you will be refunded to you in full with no deduction.

A contingency is your protection that if your requirements cannot be met, you do not have to purchase the property. If the contingencies can be met, you are bound by the agreement to complete the purchase. This is where you must be careful. When you sign a formal contract of sale, you are acknowledging in writing that you promise to fulfill certain requirements in the agreement with the intent to purchase the property.

The seller also promises to sell you the property under the agreed conditions. The seller removes the property from the market and continues to pay the mortgage, taxes, insurance, and maintenance. The seller is optimistic that you are a qualified buyer and begins to set up her own plans to move and buy a new home. Emotions begin to run a little higher.

If a contingency has been entered into the agreement by you for your protection, you are required to act on that contingency as quickly as you can, in good faith, to relieve the question as soon as possible. If the contingency cannot be met, even after **due diligence** (your best efforts), the agreement can be voided. If the contingency was not met by choice or negligence by the buyer, the seller may have cause to declare the buyer in default of the agreement and make a claim for damages. The damages may be retention of the deposit money, or the seller may have the right to sue you for **specific performance** of the agreement and force you to buy the house.

Formal contracts are legally binding agreements that allow both parties to insert the terms and conditions of the transaction. When you insert a condition into the agreement that requires certain actions on your part to be fulfilled, you are required to perform that action to the best of your ability in the shortest time possible to protect the interests of the seller. If you do not follow through with the contingency when it is possible for you to do so, you may be in default of the agreement; the seller may claim to have been damaged or financially harmed by your actions and demand compensation. Similarly, if the seller includes certain contingencies and does not act on them in good faith, you may also be able to claim a default.

A very important paragraph in the contract is the date inserted for the closing of title, or the actual day of the sale. The seller will want a definite day inserted because he must make arrangements to buy a new home and schedule his move. You also would like a target date inserted, but you need to allow yourself enough time to obtain your mortgage commitment from the lender and arrange your own finances and moving schedule.

One word in this paragraph can change the entire contract. It can read that the closing will take place at a certain place and at a certain time **on or about** a certain day, which gives you a certain amount of latitude to follow up on last-minute arrangements and finalize your requirements under the agreement. The phrase *on or about* relates to what is known as **reasonable time,** which in most states is within 30 days of the originally designated date as long as both parties to the agreement are pursuing the resolution of the contingencies in the agreement with due diligence.

For example, let's say that your contract calls for a closing within 90 days of contract signing, on or about, and the lender does not issue the commitment letter in a timely manner and schedules the closing for a date 10 days after the projected closing date in the contract. You should be protected with the on-or-about wording in the agreement, because 10 days is a reasonable time.

However, if the language is changed to read **on or before** a certain date, **the entire agreement is now considered a time-is-of-the-essence contract.** With a time-is-of-the-essence agreement, you are required to close title *on or before* that specific day and no later. If you cannot meet that requirement, you will be in default of the agreement, and the seller may have legal recourse for damages. This is where one word can have a dramatic effect on the entire agreement. Do not sign a time-is-of-the-essence agreement unless you are absolutely sure you can meet the deadline.

If you are unsure about the structure or language of a contract, make the contract signing subject to your attorney's review and approval and obtain legal advice.

WHAT ABOUT INSURANCE?

The most common homeowners policies cover the most common problems, such as

- Fire and lightning
- Windstorm and hail
- Vandalism
- Smoke and water damage
- Theft
- Explosions
- Riots or civil unrest
- Aircraft crashes into home
- Glass damage
- Ice and snow
- Damage from heating systems or sprinkler systems
- Damage caused by electrical malfunction
- Vehicles hitting the property

The average homeowner's insurance will run anywhere from $275 to about $600 per year depending on geographical location and the full value of the property. My policy costs about $350 per year for property in lower New York State.

However, if you are locating in an area that has a history of active volcanoes, earthquakes, floods, or other natural disasters, your coverage will be more expensive. Earthquake insurance costs about $1 per $1,000 of coverage, with a 10 percent deductible thrown in. This means that if your home is worth $100,000 *without the value of the land included* and it is totally destroyed in an earthquake, you are responsible for the first $10,000, and the insurance company pays the balance when you rebuild. This insurance, therefore, would cost you *at least* an additional $100 per year. The alternative, recently learned all too well in California, is to lose everything if a disaster occurs, and you still have to pay off the mortgage, even if the house no longer exists. *Coverage* does not necessarily mean coverage of the property's full value; make sure the full value expressed by the insurance company is the same or more than the actual value of the property.

It is normally required by lenders that proof of insurance be provided before the closing is scheduled. The lender will require you to purchase additional insurance to protect the lender in a disaster-prone area.

If you are located within a short distance from a firehouse or police station or there is a fire hydrant in front of the house, you may be able to negotiate a small amount off the premium. Usually the insurance companies will charge a smaller premium if you are located within 1,000 feet of a fire hydrant.

HOW MUCH INSURANCE DO I NEED?

The lender will require you to purchase enough insurance to cover at least the amount of the mortgage. If you are fortunate to be able to keep the mortgage amount to a minimum and you have equity in the home, make sure that you buy enough insurance to cover the entire investment, not just the mortgage.

Remember, whatever is not insured you will have to make up out of pocket if there is a loss. My advice is to insure the property for its full value, pay the premiums, and not have to worry about it.

If you have certain personal items of value such as jewelry, office equipment, expensive tools, a big-screen TV, or anything more valuable than normal household items, make sure the insurance covers those items.

The lender will require that you produce a copy of the original policy or at least a binder for the policy from your agent when you sign and return the commitment letter for the mortgage. Most lenders will not even schedule a closing for the financing until all the paperwork is in place and they have copies of all documents.

You will need **liability coverage** to cover the possibility of personal injury to anyone entering your property such as the neighbors' kids or even an invited guest.

Typically, this insurance offers $100,000 of coverage. However, it is a good idea to ask for an **umbrella policy** that extends this coverage to a higher number. Most often, the umbrella policy costs surprisingly less than you would think when taken in conjunction with your original policy, and it's worth it. What would you do if someone was injured on your property, sued you, and won an award for $500,000? Your insurance company would pay the first $100,000, and you would be on the hook for the balance. The umbrella rider kicks in **after** the initial $100,000 is paid to reduce your exposure even further. You will also need **property protection coverage** to protect your investment and the bank. This coverage will compensate you if the property is damaged or destroyed. However, it will not cover you against damage by earthquake, flood, or volcanoes unless you purchase that additional coverage.

Make sure that your policy has an **automatic cost-of-living increase** built in. If you have the house for several years and you originally paid $130,000 for it ($100,000 for the house and $30,000 for the land), the replacement costs to rebuild the same house could be $150,000 (not including the land). Your insurance will pay the $100,000 that is on the policy, and you will pay the balance unless you have a policy that allows for an **inflation rate** to compensate for the increase in costs.

The property coverage will also include personal items such as clothes, jewelry, automobiles, and more, but the insurance companies set certain limits for how much they will pay for certain items. If you have personal items that exceed the values offered by the insurance company, make it known that you want those items covered in full. It might cost a little more in premiums, but can you afford to take the loss? You may have to have those items appraised to verify their actual cash value before the company will agree to insure them. You have to establish whether the insurance company is offering the repay the actual cash value or the replacement costs to determine which policy suits your needs.

If you are having a problem finding a private insurance carrier, call the National Insurance Consumer Helpline at (800)942-4242 for information on how to acquire basic coverage.

If you are locating in a flood-prone area and are having a problem, call the National Flood Insurance Program (NFIP) at (800)638-6620 for help. NFIP is a federally sponsored program administered by the Federal Emergency Management Agency (FEMA).

WHERE CAN I FIND INSURANCE?

Your real estate agent should be able to help you locate a responsible insurance agent in your target area. It wouldn't hurt to ask around your new office or simply search the way you did for the property. Most major insurance companies maintain local offices, and homeowners insurance is usually the easiest insurance to obtain.

An insurance policy is a contract between you and the insurance company, explaining what it will and will not cover under certain conditions. Make sure you read the policy and understand what is and is not covered. Insurance policies are written in a way that intentionally confuses the buyer. The policies are prepared with such gobbledygook language (you can tell that this is not my strongest area) that what the words actually mean is left open to interpretation—all for the benefit of the insurance company if there is a problem.

Insurance agents make a commission when they sell a policy and look forward to the commissions on your renewal policies to secure their future. Make it understood that if you do not understand the policy, you are not going to buy it from the agent, and make him explain the language to you.

There are five basic forms of homeowners insurance labeled HO and numbered to address the extent and intent of coverage. **HO-1** is the most basic coverage, is probably not acceptable to the lender, and you wouldn't want it anyway. **HO-2** costs a little more than HO-1 but includes coverage for real problems such as broken pipes or explosions. **HO-3** is considered an **all-risk policy** and covers everything up to and including appliances and floor coverings. An **HO-3** policy will also include your liability insurance. For condominium owners, the **HO-6** policy is the one to use, and if the property is a unique, custom home or an older home of a certain style and condition, you would ask for an **HO-8** policy.

All of these policies have their own limitations of coverage. Ask the insurance agent to give you a written list of your policies' limitations. Study that list and decide whether you want more coverage for certain items.

The main areas to pay attention to are the replacement costs if the house is damaged or destroyed; how much of a deductible the company allows; how the deductible affects your premiums; how much extra money is required to cover any valuable personal items; and how much liability coverage is prudent in your new area.

16

HOMEOWNER WARRANTIES

There are hundreds of warranty programs available in most states that offer additional protection to home buyers. A homeowner warranty is simply a warranty, underwritten by an insurance company, that offers to repair or replace certain items in the home if they are found to be defective within a certain time frame.

Homeowner warranties became a big sales tool for builders selling newly constructed homes. When you buy a resale home, you can kick the tires and basically see what it is you're buying before you buy. With new construction, unless the home resembles an existing model or a similar home has been constructed on the site, you are buying a concept of a home derived from information provided by pictures on a brochure and a set of building plans.

It is difficult to sell people something they cannot see—especially something that costs many thousands of dollars and that is to be provided by a stranger. To make buyers more comfortable with their decision to buy a new home (besides the builders' own company warranty, usually good for one year), builders may offer additional protection by providing an additional warranty that can be extended up to 15 years. This makes buyers feel more comfortable with buying something that does not yet exist.

Homeowner warranties became very popular, and eventually extended home warranties were being offered for resale homes as well as for new homes; these offer buyers some protection against potential defects that were not divulged by the owner.

Homeowner warranties are limited warranties, which means that they cover only certain areas of the home for a certain time, not 100 percent of the home 100 percent of the time.

Normally the builder's own warranty will cover the entire home for the first year. The extended warranty picks up the coverage beginning with the second year and can be extended to the fifteenth year depending on how much you or the seller is willing to pay in premiums.

The seller or builder may offer a certain coverage for a certain number of years. If you want more coverage, you will be asked to pay for it yourself. Depending on the plan to which you agree, you can expect to obtain 100 percent coverage of the home for at least the first year and possibly for the second year for all workmanship and materials. After the first or second year, the coverage will be limited to plumbing, electrical, and mechanical systems. After the third year, the coverage may be limited to structural defects for the balance of the term.

In New York State, a builder must, by law, provide a minimum of six years of limited warranty before or in conjunction with any other warranties provided; in California, it is ten years. The laws will vary from state to state. The question is, If the builder goes out of business, what good is the mandatory warranty?

Certain companies offer warranties only for new construction, and others offer coverage for both new and resale homes. Warranty companies also offer arbitration services if there is a claim from a buyer. **Arbitration** means that instead of calling your attorney and starting a lengthy and expensive law suit, representatives from the warranty companies will offer to sit down between you and the seller to try to work out the problem.

Most warranty companies take their business very seriously and will screen a builder very carefully to establish the builder's credibility before accepting it into the warranty program. Similarly, before the warranty company will accept a resale home into the program, an engineer must inspect the home to establish its integrity as an acceptable risk. If it is found that the seller is responsible for the defect, the warranty company will work with you to entice the seller to correct the problem before a law suit needs to be filed.

A typical homeowners warranty for new homes will cover items during the first year such as

- Excavating and back filling the foundation and trenches
- Site drainage, including drains and swales
- Water infiltration of crawlspaces
- All concrete work, including expansion and contraction joints
- Cast-in-place concrete, such as basement walls, floors, and exterior steps
- All masonry work, including masonry siding
- Rough carpentry, including framing, floors, squeaks, and depressions
- Finished carpentry (interior and exterior), including all interior trim and moldings
- Wood treatment for delamination or deterioration of siding and floors
- Waterproofing basements and crawlspaces or slabs
- Insulation sufficiency
- Singles and roof tiles for leaks, including all vents and louvers
- All roofing and siding (and all flashing material), including ice buildup and wind-driven rain
- Flat built-up roofing, including damage caused by standing water
- All flashing and sheet metal material, including gutters and downspouts
- All sealant materials, for leaks due to improper caulking
- Wood and plastic doors, for warping or peeling
- Wood, metal, and plastic windows, for air and water leakage and warping
- Weather stripping and seals, for cracking

- All finishes for Sheetrock, lathe, and plaster
- All ceramic tile for loose or cracked tile
- All flooring, for nail pops, depressions, bubbles, shrinkage, or gaps
- All carpeting, for loose and separating seams
- Any special coatings such as exterior stucco surfaces or parged foundation walls
- All painting, for mildew or fungus, stains or peeling, or simple deterioration
- All wall coverings, even wallpaper, for peeling or bubbles
- All louvers and vents of basements, attics, and crawlspaces
- All fireplaces, for proper installation of chimneys and potential separation from shrinking
- All cabinets and countertops in the kitchen and baths, for warping and peeling
- All water supply systems, including all waste drains, for leaking and freezing and proper operation
- Septic system design, installation, and operation
- All plumbing pipes, fixtures, and valves, including noisy pipes and leaks
- Heating systems
- Cooling systems
- Condensation lines, against clogging
- Evaporative cooling systems, for proper operation
- Air distribution systems, including noisy ductwork
- All electrical systems including all conductors, switches, and receptacles

You can see from this list that the house is covered thoroughly and that the seller or builder must agree that each of these items functions properly.

Resale warranties are similar but differ in that they provide coverage for certain items only after a complete inspection has been performed to verify that the items to be insured are not faulty to begin with.

HOW DO I OBTAIN A WARRANTY?

If you are buying a newly constructed home, the builder may offer a separate insurance-backed warranty package as an incentive for you to buy. If you are buying a resale house, you can make the extended warranty a part of the negotiations to buy. In certain cases, the seller will be willing to pay all or a portion of the insurance premiums. In other cases the real estate agent may offer to pay a portion of the premiums, or you may be able to pay the premiums yourself.

Ask the sales agent for a list of companies that offer homeowner warranties in your area. If the agent cannot provide this information, ask your home insurance agent or ask several agents to try to find the company that offers the best policy.

If the home is several years old or more, a homeowner's warranty is not a bad idea. Remember, every system in the house grows old and wears out eventually. If any part of the house contains a defect, you will pay for the repair if you don't have a warranty.

For more information on warranties, write to the National Home Warranty Association, 498 Thorndale Drive, #200, Buffalo Grove, IL 60089 to receive its *Guide to Home Warranties for Consumers and Real Estate Professionals* free of charge.

HOW MUCH DOES A WARRANTY COST?

In the Northeast, the average cost for a homeowner warranty will run from $300 to $500 for the first year's coverage and less per year thereafter if you want extended coverage. You must decide how long the coverage should run and how much you (or the seller) are willing to pay for it.

I feel that the peace of mind that an extended warranty offers you by protecting you against unforeseen problems is worth the price.

DO I NEED A WARRANTY?

The choice is yours (isn't it always?) to buy an extended warranty or not. If the house is several years old and was built with quality materials and labor, you may consider an extended warranty for just the septic system or heating and cooling systems. If the house is structurally sound, you must inspect the various systems in the house for wear and tear to determine if additional protection is needed.

If the house is new, the builder will offer its warranty, at which time you should let the builder know that if it pays for an extended warranty, you would feel better about buying that new house.

══ 17 ══

FINALLY...THE CLOSING

Congratulations, you have survived the ordeal and won! Take a moment to reflect back on all that you have accomplished so far. You have

- Identified the various buyer groups
- Learned why people buy
- Qualified the benefits of ownership
- Identified the various forms of housing
- Qualified the style and size of home you need
- Qualified the financing for the property
- Identified the various forms of lenders
- Identified the various forms of financing
- Learned the appraisal process
- Qualified the location of a property
- Qualified the house and the land
- Qualified a real-estate sales agent
- Qualified an attorney
- Learned about radon and EMF radiation

- Learned about wells and septic systems
- Learned about surveys and topography
- Learned the title process and forms of title
- Learned what zoning is and how it affects property
- Learned about purchase offers and formal contracts
- Obtained hints on insurance and warranties

It is time to pat yourself on the back. You may not be a practicing real estate professional, but you know as much or more than many of those presently working in the field about the most important aspects of the business.

Now it is time to bring all of that effort to the final reward— buying a house.

WHEN AND WHERE?

When you signed the formal contract of sale, you should have seen a paragraph that designates the location, date, and time for the closing. This paragraph explains that the closing will take place on or about the target day for the projected closing. When the bank issued the letter of commitment, it specified a certain number of days that it will hold the mortgage amount and interest rate without requiring a new application. The contract and commitment letter should also designate the address where the closing will take place, usually in a conference room at the lender's office or the office of the attorney for the lender.

When you receive your commitment letter from the lender, you will see a list of items that the lender requires before the closing date can be set. The lender generally will not set the date for the closing until all of the items on the commitment letter have been delivered to the lender to complete its files. Often, the lender may require additional material that did not appear on the commitment letter. It is the sales agent's responsibility to follow up with the lender on a regular basis to make sure the file doesn't sit there waiting for another document. It is your responsibility to follow up with the sales agent and the lender to make sure the process is moving along. Remember, you are under the gun to perform your obligations under the contract. Call the lender at least once a week to verify that it has everything it needs to complete the mortgage. If it needs another document, maybe a well certification or a copy of the house inspection, possibly a copy of the survey or deed, supply that document as quickly as you can. Your file will sit on the back burner until the lenders file is complete.

Once the file is ready, the lender's mortgage-processing department sends the file to the lender's attorney for scheduling. Don't be surprised if the closing is scheduled several weeks after the file has been completed. The attorneys are usually busy and must schedule closings weeks in advance. Depending on the time of year, you may find that the lender's attorney, your attorney, or the seller's attorney is on vacation—great for them, but you have to close title on time.

It is not uncommon for one or more of the attorneys to be extremely busy or out of town. Raise your voice and demand that another attorney with the firm represent you at the closing. If your attorney is the one holding things up, try to work it out. If you cannot, hire another attorney at a reduced fee to handle the closing. All the work has been done; all this attorney needs to do is show up and verify that all is as it should be at the closing.

If you are not using an attorney and the escrow company is handling the closing, continue to push for a definite closing date. If the escrow company needs additional information, don't rely on the broker or escrow company to obtain it; go get it yourself and deliver it to the escrow company. Get it done!

WHAT TO DO BEFORE THE CLOSING

Once you have a definite time, day, and place for the closing and you have verified that everyone who needs to be there is coming (make sure your attorney notifies your title company about the closing, as it is not unusual for attorneys to forget them), there are a few simple things you should attend to.

Make sure that your attorney notifies the title company that this is a title closing, not simply a mortgage closing. It happens.

Make sure that you have your moving company coordinated. Contact the seller and make sure that his schedule is coordinated with yours and that everyone knows who is doing what. You don't want to show up with your moving company at the same time the seller's moving company shows up to move him.

Verify that everything that the seller agreed to leave with the house remains with the house. If you review this list with the seller a week or so before the closing, it will be hard for him to forget and pack those items with him.

Verify that you have all the cash you will need for the closing. Ask your attorney for a breakdown of expenses you are expected to pay. Your attorney should have received a closing statement from the seller's attorney regarding items such as fuel remaining in the tank, personal items for which you negotiated, property tax adjustments, and so on. Your attorney should have a good idea of what the lender will require, such as a full-year property-tax escrow; any additional points or bank fees payable at closing; or additional interest charges to complete the current month, with the actual mortgage payments beginning within 30 to 45 days. You want to know how much money you will need to close the title, move into the home, and have enough left over for hot dogs and beans.

Make sure your insurance agent has the insurance policy ready. Notify the power company to turn off your existing power and turn on the power at the new home as of the day of the closing. Do the same with the oil or gas company to ensure continued fuel for heat and hot water. Notify the post office of your forwarding address and pick up several packets of change-of-address cards. Notify the water company with the same information. Make sure you have the kids registered with the new school. Notify the telephone company. Call the mover, the lender's attorney, and your attorney to verify that all is ready. Have some wine!!

Arrange for the final walk-through with the sales agent and the seller, which usually happens the day before or the morning of the closing, to verify that all is as it should be with the property.

WHAT TO BRING WITH YOU

Everyone who is to be named on the deed and signed on the mortgage must attend the closing. If you have a cosignor for the note and mortgage, make sure he or she is ready. Bring your checkbook and make sure that you have enough checks. If the balance of the purchase price (over the mortgage amount) is to be paid by bank or certified check, make sure the check and the amount are correct. Bring your copies of the original purchase agreement and the formal contract and all of your notes just in case there is a question or a problem that needs verification. If you can arrange it, **do not bring young children to the closing.** They are unable to sit still, and you need to pay attention to what you are signing. Your attorney, the seller's attorney, and the lender's attorney will bring everything else. It is a good idea to meet with your attorney about an hour before the closing to go over any final questions.

DURING THE CLOSING

You will be expected to sign the **mortgage note** or **bond** guaranteeing the repayment of the mortgage. You will sign the **actual mortgage document.** You will sign the **RESPA (Real Estate Settlement Procedures Act) form** to acknowledge that you understand the procedure and that no one is taking advantage of you. You may be required to sign a **truth-in-lending form** to verify to the bank that the mortgage costs, principal, and interest have been explained to you. You may be asked to sign a copy of the settlement charges and closing costs breakdown, and you definitely will be asked to sign many checks. You might also be asked to sign an affidavit to acknowledge that you have used no other name than the one you are presently using for at least 10 years, and you may be asked to provide picture identification to prove you are who you claim to be.

Figure 17-1 shows a list of settlement and closing costs. Go over this list with your attorney before the closing to verify your understanding of what expenses you will incur on closing day. Obtain copies from the lender.

When you get to the closing, make sure you take the time to shake hands with the seller, the seller's attorney, the bank attorney, the real estate agent, and the title attorney and introduce those who have accompanied you. Most of the people in the room will be meeting you for the first time, and you want to make a good impression. If a problem arises, you will be the

Loan discount points (if not already paid)	$_____
Loan origination fee (if not already paid)	$_____
Credit report fee	$_____
Appraisal fee	$_____
Lender's inspection fee	$_____
Mortgage insurance application	$_____
Prorated interest (interest charged daily until principal payments begin)	$_____
Homeowners insurance premium	$_____
Mortgage insurance premium (for PMI)	$_____
Property tax escrow	$_____
Mortgage recording fee	$_____
Mortgage tax (if any)	$_____
Bank attorney fee (if any)	$_____
Lender's title policy (if required)	$_____

TITLE CLOSING COSTS

Cash balance over financing	$_____
Title policy fee	$_____
Notary or your attorney's fee	$_____
Recording fee for deed	$_____
Pest inspection fee (if not already paid)	$_____
Engineer's report (if not already paid)	$_____
Certified survey fee	$_____
Adjustments with the seller for fuel or other items	$_____
Total These Numbers and Buy a Lottery Ticket ASAP. TOTAL	$_____

Figure 17-1.   Mortgage settlement closing costs.

"good guy" who was kind enough to shake hands and greet everyone in the room. Everyone likes to help the good guys.

Another little trick I use is to place my checkbook and certified checks in the middle of the table facing the seller. This makes the seller confident that you have the money to consummate the transaction and also gives him or her something to think about. The seller is just as anxious to close and receive the money as you are to pay it and own the house. However, sometimes a problem comes up with the seller or between the attorneys, who like to challenge each other once in a while. I have found that the seller will constantly glance at the checks and checkbook throughout the proceedings, and if a problem comes up, the seller may be in a more progressive frame of mind to resolve the problem with all of that money staring him in the face.

If a problem arises, reach over and slide the checks toward you and keep your hand on them until the problem is resolved; then slide them back. Get the picture? Occasionally, a question comes up that may or may not have been previously discussed and agreed to, and everyone's face gets that classic "who, me?" look. Most often the discussion revolves around an item worth no more and frequently less than several hundred dollars, and after the cacophony of gibberish dies down, everyone looks at the buyer and seller with raised eyebrows. This is where you are down to the nitty-gritty, and what happens next depends on how much you want or need this house.

Occasionally, the seller or the seller's attorney will create such a situation to play hero and squeeze that little extra out of the buyer. Sometimes buyers play this game, and sometimes it is a legitimate oversight. Whatever the circumstance, if you really want or need this house and your back is against the wall, you should try to compromise and split the bill with the seller. If you are adamant that you will not pay a penny more, throw a raised eyebrow look at the real estate agent and see if she is willing to pay a portion of the disputed amount. If that fails, be prepared to gather up everything and walk out of the room.

Believe me, when you start putting your files away, sliding the checks off the table, and putting on your coat, all hell is going to break loose. Your attorney will ask to speak with you alone in the hallway (that is what attorneys do). Simply be honest with yourself about whether you are prepared to follow through. Usually, when everyone thinks that the entire deal will fall through and no one will get what they came for (in other words, no one is going to get paid), somebody comes up with a solution that will satisfy the problem.

If not, and the problem is severe enough to warrant killing the deal, walk out, go to the nearest bar, and offer a toast to yourself that you were strong enough to walk away from it all. But remember, you still need a house, and you will have to start the process all over—is it really worth it? Also, there may be lawsuits against you for not completing your end of the transaction. **If you walk out, be prepared to live with that decision.**

I'll close this chapter with descriptions of the various forms you will see at the closing. The language on these forms will vary so as to allow the various state laws to be incorporated, but the basics should be the same. Ask your lender to provide you with blank copies to help you understand what they do.

THE MORTGAGE

The mortgage is considered a **security instrument** that describes the borrower, the lender, and the property. Also included are explanations and descriptions of the following topics:

1. The borrower's transfer to lender of rights in the property, in the event of a default
2. A legal description of the property
3. The borrower's right to mortgage the property and the borrower's obligation to defend ownership of the property
4. A plain language security agreement
5. The borrower's promise to pay
6. Monthly payments for taxes and insurance (borrower's obligation)
7. Application of the borrower's payments, used to pay the mortgage
8. The borrower's obligation to pay charges, assessments, and claims pertaining to water, sewer, and similar services
9. The borrower's obligation to maintain hazard and property insurance
10. The borrower's obligation to occupy the property, maintain and protect the property, and fulfill any lease obligations
11. The lender's rights to protect its rights in the property, in the event of a default on the loan
12. Mortgage insurance and a promise to pay the premiums
13. The lender's right to inspect the property at reasonable times

14. Agreements about condemnation of the property (In the event of condemnation, you promise to use the condemnation award to pay off the lender first.)

15. Continuation of borrower's obligations and lender's rights, (Make sure, in the event of an assumption when you sell, that you are no longer signed on the mortgage and note.)

16. Loan charges (If the charges relating to this loan are considered unlawful, you are due a refund.)

17. Notices required under this security agreement (If you change your address or there is a problem with the property, you are required to notify the lender by mail.)

18. Law that governs this security agreement, which relates to federal and state laws incorporated into the agreement

19. Borrower's copy (You are entitled to copies of the note and mortgage.)

20. Agreements about the lender's rights if the property is sold or transferred (The mortgage may be "callable," or payable in full, if the property is sold.)

21. The borrower's right to have the lender's enforcement of this security instrument discontinued (If the loan is paid on time and paid off, the lender must release you from this mortgage by filing a satisfaction of lien with the county clerk.)

22. The note holder's right to sell the note or an interest in the note; the borrower's right to notice of change of loan service (You have the right to be notified in the event the lender sells the note, which is the norm these days.)

23. Continuation of borrower's obligations to maintain and protect the property (Deals with environmental laws, flammable liquids, and so on.)

24. The lender's rights if the borrower fails to keep promises (They have the right to call the loan and foreclose on the property.)

25. The lender's obligation to discharge this security agreement (The lender must file the satisfaction when the lien is paid.)

26. Agreements regarding the state lien laws (There may be a rider attached to this agreement that further specifies the above details subject to state law.)

THE MORTGAGE NOTE

This form is your promise to repay the loan. The borrower, lender, and property address are included. Also included are the principal amount borrowed and the interest rate charged. The following topics are also included:

1. Payments, designating the day the payments begin and the day they end

2. The borrower's right to prepay (This specifies your right to make additional payments to reduce the principal amount at any time without penalty, with the provision that the payments remain the same with the interest adjusted to the reduced principal amount.)

3. Loan charges (This sets forth the legality of the charges and specifies that any overcharges will be refunded to you.)

4. The borrower's failure to pay as required (This sets forth the grace period allowed before you incur late charges and specifies the amount to be charged. It states that your failure to pay the loan will be a default; sets the time limit to make up the payments; and states that if you default, the note holder has the right to call the entire debt due and payable.)

5. No waiver by note holder (Even if the note holder does not require payment in full, it holds the right to do so at a later date.)

6. Giving notice (Any notices to you must be sent by first-class mail.)

7. Obligations of persons under this note (This restates your obligations under the note, and any others who may sign the note have the same obligations individually. If you have a cosignor to the note, each person is individually responsible for the terms of the note, whether one or the other pays the debts or not.)

8. Waivers (These waive the rights of *presentment* and *dishonor.* Notice of presentment means you waive your right to require that the note holder make demands for payment [it doesn't have to chase you]. Notice of dishonor means you have the right to require the note holder to give notice to any other persons obligated under this agreement.)

9. Uniform security code (This states that the note is a uniform instrument that may vary with jurisdictions and relates to the mortgage, deed of trust, or security deed that further describes the loan obligation. Further, the lender's rights if the property is sold or transferred, where the lender may require payment in full, are explained.)

TRUTH-IN-LENDING DISCLOSURE FOR REAL ESTATE MORTGAGE LOANS

This form will contain information regarding the name and address of both borrower and lender. The annual percentage rate (APR), total interest charged, the principal amount financed, and the total amount of principal and interest payments are stated.

The loan is broken down by the number and amount of the required payments and when they are to begin and end. The type of loan is described, whether it be fixed rate or variable rate. It sets forth how the loan is secured (by the property), the cost for any late charges, whether prepayment of the loan will have a penalty, and whether the loan is assumable or not.

DISCLOSURE FORM

The disclosure form also sets forth the annual percentage rate and explains that the points are included in the overall rate. It explains that the interest is calculated over the life of the loan, including points and PMI.

Also explained is the total amount financed, including all principal, interest, points, and private mortgage insurance.

OWNER'S ESTOPPEL CERTIFICATE

This form certifies to the lender that the mortgage is a first mortgage and a first lien on the property. The property address, loan amount, loan payment schedule, and loan interest are stated. Reference is made to the mortgage and mortgage note.

COMPLIANCE AGREEMENT

This is another promise by you that you will comply with all requests to furnish the lender any further information it needs regarding your mortgage application, and you certify that all of the information provided on the application is true. You again promise to abide by the terms of the mortgage and note.

RESPA FORM

This is a federal requirement. The Real Estate Settlement and Procedures Act (RESPA) requires lenders to have you acknowledge that you have been instructed as to how the closing process works, what all of the documentation means and does, and further, that you fully understand your financial obligations regarding the mortgage.

You will also receive invoices from the title company for the title policy, from the lender's attorney for its fee, from your attorney for her fee, and for your homeowner's insurance (if not already paid). The lender will probably require a tax escrow account to ensure that the property taxes are paid on time. It may require up to one year's taxes in advance.

Remember, in certain western states closed in escrow through escrow companies, you are not entitled to take possession of the premises until the closing documents have been recorded in the county records, usually several days after the closing. Verify this with your broker and escrow company.

You will receive a closing statement from the seller's attorney setting forth the balance due and any fuel and tax adjustments due the seller. The seller's attorney will ask the seller to sign the property over to you by signing the deed. The title company will take the deed and have it recorded in the county clerk's office. After it is recorded, it is sent back to your attorney or to you. And you're done—you have writer's cramp, you're broke, but you're happy. You now have the most important item of all—the keys. Congratulations, you made it—your new title is homeowner!

INDEX